Tomorrow's God

Tomorrow's God

The Hebrew Lord in an Age of Science

Robert N. Goldman

EDITED BY
Mary L. Radnofsky

PREFACE BY
Judith Ann Goldman

*For Jim —
Thanks for the music
of my life!
Mary Radnofsky
2014*

WIPF & STOCK · Eugene, Oregon

TOMORROW'S GOD
The Hebrew Lord in an Age of Science

Copyright © 2019 Judith Ann Goldman. All rights reserved. Except for brief quotations in critical publications or reviews, no part of this book may be reproduced in any manner without prior written permission from the publisher. Write: Permissions, Wipf and Stock Publishers, 199 W. 8th Ave., Suite 3, Eugene, OR 97401.

Wipf & Stock
An Imprint of Wipf and Stock Publishers
199 W. 8th Ave., Suite 3
Eugene, OR 97401

www.wipfandstock.com

PAPERBACK ISBN: 978-1-5326-7464-8
HARDCOVER ISBN: 978-1-5326-7465-5
EBOOK ISBN: 978-1-5326-7466-2

Quotations reprinted from *Tanakh: The Holy Scriptures*, by permission of the University of Nebraska Press. Copyright 1985 by the Jewish Publication Society, Philadelphia.

Manufactured in the U.S.A.   09/13/19

In Loving Memory
Robert N. Goldman
1926–2005

As long as you pray to God and ask him for something,
you are not a religious man.

—ALBERT EINSTEIN[1]

1. Calaprice, *Ultimate Quotable Einstein,* 343. As expressed to and quoted by Leo Szilard. Commentator's note: Robert Goldman used the earlier edition: Calaprice, *Expanded Quotable Einstein.*

Contents

Foreword

SCIENTIFIC DISCOVERIES HAVE LONG inspired artists, philosophers, and poets to look out at the world and share its wonder in a new light. Scientific thinking has also encouraged us to look inward at the depths of ourselves—our physical, spiritual, individual, and collective selves—in evolving ways and to ponder what we've accomplished or may someday become. For thousands of years on this uniquely human journey, we've also struggled to understand the nature of existence. We've explored our connections with divergent cultures, places, and people. We've tried to understand relationships with family, each other, and God.

Perhaps the most difficult relationship to understand is the one that "I" have with "Myself." Who am "I?" A man? A woman? Black, white, brown? Am I unique, even if I have a twin? If I change my appearance or gender, does my old "self" change, or will I always be the same "self" that I was born?

Research and inventions have further permitted striking opportunities for humans to discover who we are—as a species and as individuals. For example, in the Human Genome Project, we've mapped the uniquely sequenced billions of gene pairs in a single person. Medical and social advances allow us to be seen by others the way we perceive ourselves. And though it's possible to find mutations on DNA to identify pathologies such as Alzheimer's—a disease that seems to change one's sense of self—the world still does not agree on just what "self" is. Fortunately, Bob Goldman reflected on this question, researched it from religious, spiritual, philosophical, and scientific perspectives, then wrote this book to help the rest of us figure it out.

Understanding who "I" am, of course, goes far beyond grammar of the first-person pronoun. Some people say "I" to designate their identity as speaker or as member of a group, while others say "I," knowing with certainty there's a different "self" within them—possibly of a different gender or race. This highlights one aspect of the complex question of who I am, regardless of whom I may appear to be. So Bob takes the reader on an exploration of the question, "Who Am I?" not only to raise awareness of one's self-identity in a crowded, busy world, but to better understand human relationships with each other and with a "Higher Self."

While academics have argued meaning in the countless Bible translations, this book instead engages the reader in dialogue with Bob Goldman—a scientist, family man, and self-made scholar/teacher who doesn't claim to have all the answers but who wants to explore questions of identity, beliefs, relationships, words, knowledge, perception, and God across cultures, space, and time. Bob discusses the human self through scientists, philosophers, and theologians, while speaking to the reader in his own, natural voice. To his delight, as he studied and made scientific discoveries, Bob came to find that, as humanity evolves, so does the human self. He considered such evolution inevitable and believed that the human self will continue to evolve, reflecting God.

Bob also found the entire concept of God to be evolving, as he shows in the emerging relationship of ancient Jews with their Hebrew Lord, and in the form of Einstein's theories of relativity—both of which explain the complex interaction between existence, being, self, and time. According to Bob, it is humanity's responsibility to continue such scientific thinking and personal evolution, to move us toward a higher understanding of the self, and thus toward a higher level of consciousness. In other words, the more we learn, the closer we get to God.

Not expecting everyone to simply accept this reasoning, Bob develops his thesis logically and patiently, anticipating questions a reader might use to challenge him: How can we know if a greater Self exists? How would a greater Self help us as individuals, or as all humanity?

Bob also provides metaphors to illuminate relationships: for example, the ancient Hebrews viewed time differently from modern Western society; they accepted the past, present, and future all as "real." In contrast, today, we see the past as finished and the future as not yet existing.

So what did this coexistence of the past, present, and future look like for the ancients? Well, imagine you're rowing a boat on the water. In a rowboat, you face backwards and see where you've been. In other words, you can see your own past. Your back is in the direction the boat is moving, and although you can't see your future until you get there, you're on a constant journey towards it. Rowing steadily, you're in an ever-changing present, your oars constantly pulling the boat along. Thus, all these moments in time are real and relevant to you.

And what about eternity? Well, by reading this book, you may discover your own evolving relationship with God, time, and existence. Perhaps, as I hope, you'll also gain new appreciation of the precious life moments you personally get to experience—such as reading this book.

So, discover your own questions. And enjoy.

Mary L. Radnofsky, Ph.D.

Editor

Preface

Happy is the man who finds wisdom and attains understanding.

We read to learn, to be enlightened and informed, to be entertained, to laugh, to see the world through another's eyes. Although published posthumously, and by an author probably unfamiliar, the book you hold in your hand does all of the above and more. It may change your understanding of God, of science, of yourself. After reading it, you may look differently at your connection to the people in your life and the people you love who have died.

Robert Goldman—"Bob" to family and friends—spent his life reading extensively in the realms of computers, science, religion, and philosophy, as well as science fiction and math puzzles, and he gained wisdom. He led an active, involved life that embodied his philosophy—in his interactions with his family, friends, and community and in his work. He left the world a better place.

Whenever we know the author of a work personally, we hear his or her voice in the writing. I believe that you, too, will hear Bob's dry humor, his sarcasm, his empathy, and his admiration for original thinkers (whether he agreed with them or not), as he sought to understand and reconcile science and God.

Bringing this manuscript to light and life is my final love letter to Bob. His book is intended for the lay reader who is curious, concerned about "Life," God, and how to think about and cope with personal loss and the chaos of the world in which we live. We all seek a deeper understanding at various times in our lives, yet most of us don't really know how to approach such a task on our own. Those with extensive training in philosophy or science may have a more detailed vocabulary for certain phenomena, but we must all spend time sorting out the complex notion of who we are as individuals in an evolving relation with others and with God.

I believe Bob's book helps each of us focus more clearly on these questions by accounting for the perspectives of ancient Hebrews, modern philosophers, and scientists as we try to sift through today's flood of information to better understand our selves and each other. Each person who reads this book will be in dialog with Bob: arguing, agreeing, challenging. Bob did not accept what he read and heard without careful thought, nor should the reader.

Robert Norman Goldman was born March 28, 1926, in Providence, Rhode Island, youngest of five (fourth son) of James and Frances Goldman. Bob was strongly influenced by his Jewish immigrant parents: his father's entrepreneurial business model; his parents' volunteer and financial commitment to the local Jewish orphanage, hospital, and several synagogues; and his parents' unconditional love and support of their children.

Bob first attended Cornell University in 1943 but left at the end of his freshman year to enlist in the U.S. Navy. Although he never saw action in a war zone, he learned the latest in electrical engineering and the use of computers along with the chores of an enlisted man. When the war ended and his tour was over, he returned to Cornell to earn his engineering degree.

Always curious and inventive, his first adventure after college was developing a hydroponic tomato farm in Florida with a college buddy. He always claimed they grew the biggest and best tomatoes he ever tasted. He later moved to New York City for an engineering job with Bendix Computers, which then took him to Los Angeles, California. Computer technology was still in its early stages in 1960 when he and his business partner, Ron Katz, left Bendix to establish Telecredit, the first check-guarantee business. They utilized room-sized IBM computers to provide immediate online authorization for supermarkets and other businesses that cashed checks for their customers' convenience. This technology led to further exploration of the use of computers to benefit consumers as well as businesses. For example, among Bob's thirty-five computer system patents was the first device for reading and writing on a magnetic strip. This innovation was foundational to credit card technology.

When Bob and I met in 1962, we were both members of an outdoor camping and ski club. We married two years later. In the late 1960s, we joined the Brandeis Institute (later the Brandeis-Bardin Institute and now a retreat center of American Jewish University), which offered adults the opportunity to combine Shabbat observance with the intellectual challenges of prominent Jewish scholars-in-residence such as Elie Wiesel z"l. It was in this setting that Bob first gave a commentary on the Torah portion of the week, sharing his ideas on Torah, God, and science, and getting feedback from others.[1]

In 1972, Bob chose to leave his full-time positions with the companies he helped establish and we moved to Oʻahu, Hawaiʻi, with our young daughters, Lita and Erica. He continued as a consultant through the 1980s, then decided to allow more time for family and for exploring his interests in artificial intelligence, Albert Einstein, and religious philosophy.

His interest in Einstein led us to a family summer in Princeton, New Jersey, in the mid-1970s. Bob had received permission to access hundreds of Einstein's personal and professional letters from the Institute for Advanced Studies. He spent long days in the same building where Einstein once worked, painstakingly scouring the documents. (Today, these sources are readily available online and in published books.) The book that resulted from that research is *Einstein's God: Albert Einstein's Quest as a Scientist and as a Jew to Replace a Forsaken God*, published in 1997.

The seeds of the present book germinated decades ago and developed as Bob was writing *Einstein's God*. At the same time, in all fields of science, particularly in physics and computer technology, knowledge was advancing rapidly, so Bob continued his self-education in these areas.

Bob wasn't simply an avid reader; books were integral in his life. He always had a book in his hand or his pocket. One of Bob's favorite pastimes was exploring bookstores everywhere we went. In the 1990s, we visited London often and Bob could not walk past a bookstore, especially one with used books, without stopping to look inside. While he browsed extensively, he bought selectively. He was delighted when he found a gem he could use in his writings. A few years after he died, as I was packing to move from our home, it did not surprise me to discover that our home library encompassed an estimated 10,000 volumes! It also explains why, although Bob documented his sources carefully, there are some references I was not able to find. Wherever possible, I included substitutions as close to the intent of the original as possible.

Bob was known in our Hawaiʻi Jewish community to be brilliant, but he never offered his ideas and insights gratuitously, nor did he ever

---

1. Two of Bob's commentaries were included in Bleiweiss, *Torah at Brandeis Institute,* 23, 34.

demean others. The first time I recall hearing him speak of Einstein's and the ancient Hebrews' concept of time was in 1971, when he was consoling me after the death of my father. Bob's manner and clear explanations were reassuring and comforting.

After Bob's death in 2005, a nephew told me that a conversation with Bob had revived his belief in God and Judaism. Others told me they had asked him complex questions of concern to them, and Bob always took the time to offer answers in straightforward language. He always had time to talk with his daughters or me on any topic when we had concerns or problems to solve.

As a member of Congregation Sof Ma'arav, a lay-led Conservative Jewish congregation in Honolulu, Bob had many opportunities to share and explore his ideas with others. Our congregation has a tradition of members providing commentaries (a lay-person's version of a sermon) on Shabbat and the Jewish High Holidays. Bob's comments presented on Yom Kippur for many years are still remembered by those who heard them. This book incorporates many ideas that were first shared in that setting.

On a personal level, Bob was a kind and gentle man. Family came first. We traveled often with our daughters to visit extended family. He was more introvert than extrovert, but he thoroughly enjoyed good conversation (especially when accompanied by good food and wine) with friends.

He completed this manuscript shortly before he died. Its influence on those who read it convinced me that his ideas could make a difference in people's lives and in their perceptions of Judaism and God. He may have left questions unanswered for the reader, but he also left countless opportunities for exploration in the many sources he referenced.

By looking at both traditional Jewish thinking and today's science with new eyes, Bob invited us to join him in seeing his vision. It is now my honor and my joy to share this vision with you.

Judith Goldman

A Woman's Meditation (excerpt)

God is the force of motion and light in the universe;
God is the strength of life on our planet;
God is the power moving us to do good;
God is the source of love springing up in us;
God is far beyond what we can comprehend.[2]

2. Brin, *Harvest*, 2.

Acknowledgments

WHILE THE EXPERIENCE OF writing is a solitary endeavor, bringing a manuscript to publication is not. Bob talked with people over the years whose insight and ideas made their way into this book. On his behalf—thank you.

To those who read this book in its various stages, your time and input are a gift to me and to Bob. Two longtime friends we first met at Congregation Sof Ma'arav are Robert Littman and Jordan Popper. They knew Bob and his ideas well and were generous in their support as I moved through this process. Other talented, knowledgeable friends read an early draft of the manuscript: Heather Cattell, Peter Hoffenberg, Steven Levinson, Fran Margulies, and Avi Soifer. Erica Goldman and Nanette Kaaumoana reviewed the final draft. Any errors or omissions are my own.

Todah rabah to Eve Shere and Reginald Worthley, encouraging and willing listeners as well as my best cheerleaders; to O'ahu Jewish 'Ohana Torah Study group; and to Rabbi Janet Madden, Rabbi Peter Schaktman, and Chaplain Muriel Dance.

Three people who did not know Bob were essential in the process. They came into my life at the right time. I call it *beshert,* a Yiddish word meaning connection to an event or person that is meant to be. Mary Radnofsky gave me the confidence to pursue publication. During the editing process, when Mary would say "I hear his voice" or "I imagine him chuckling," I knew meeting her was *beshert.*

When I needed a copy editor, Lee Motteler was recommended to me by the University of Hawai'i Press. Within weeks of my contacting Lee, Kīlauea Volcano near his home on the Big Island of Hawai'i began erupting. The ground was literally shaking as he worked on the manuscript! I greatly appreciate his professional skill but also his insights, patience, and positive response to Bob's writing.

Matthew Wimer, my editor, and publishers Wipf & Stock took a chance on me and on Bob, and for that trust I am extremely grateful. Marilyn Price, educator, storyteller, coauthor of *From Gratitude to Blessings and*

Back, came to Hawai'i for a weekend with my other congregation, O'ahu Jewish 'Ohana. She spoke highly of her experience with Wipf & Stock, and so another unexpected, *beshert* connection was made.

A remarkable event occurred while preparing this manuscript for publication that is unprecedented and relevant: the first photograph of a black hole was shown to the public on April 10, 2019. It is visual confirmation, based on data gathered in 2017, of Einstein's general theory of relativity. What Bob would have most appreciated is the more than 200 scientists around the world, great minds working in collaboration to achieve this outcome. Among the telescopes utilized were two in Hawai'i, and so a Hawaiian language professor named the black hole "Pōwehi," which means "the adorned fathomless dark source of unending creation." The word comes from an eighteenth-century Hawaiian chant reflecting "how deeply the Hawaiians were thinking and understanding the universe" (Jessica Dempsey, codiscoverer, *Honolulu Star-Advertiser,* 4/11/19).

Bob's vision was one of people working together to eventually, in the far distant future and in sync with his concept of YHWH, evolve to create a better world. Assuming the simultaneity of past, present, and future, I picture Albert Einstein and Bob Goldman celebrating this moment!

Always in our minds, Bob while writing and I when working toward publishing his words, have been our children—Lita, Erica, Peter, and Benjamin. Lita helped us see the world from a different perspective and pushed us to look within ourselves as well as outside the proverbial box for new ideas. Erica is her father's daughter: thoughtful, intelligent, persistent, concerned and involved with the world around her, but she puts family first. Peter is the son-in-law who had too few years to know Bob but pointed me in the right direction when I got bogged down with the immensity of this process. Benji carries his grandfather's name and is like him in so many ways: curious about the world, caring of others, bright, energetic, as well as a "chill" (his Mom's term) and loving personality. They are our inspiration.

To all who supported Bob and me through this transformative process: my deepest thanks and gratitude. You have made this effort a true community endeavor, bringing everyone closer together in ways that Bob would have loved.

Introduction

I thank the Lord a thousand times that he let me become an atheist.[1]

—GEORG CHRISTOPH LICHTENBERG (1742–1799)

AS A FRESHMAN AT Cornell many years ago, I came across a book published in 1896 by its first president, Andrew Dickson White: *The History of the Warfare of Science with Theology in Christendom*. White, together with Ezra Cornell, had founded the university twenty-nine years earlier. Their stated goal was to build a secular institution free to pursue truth without deference to existing dogma. White's book was a notable by-product. In the flowery language of that period, he introduced it in the following way:

> I simply try to aid in letting the light of historical truth into that decaying mass of outworn thought which attaches the modern world to mediaeval conceptions of Christianity and which still lingers among us—a most serious barrier to religion and morals, and a menace to the whole normal evolution of society . . . .
>
> My hope is to aid—even if it be but a little—in the gradual and healthful dissolving away of the mass of unreason, [so] that the stream of religion, pure and undefiled, may flow on broad and clear, a blessing to humanity.[2]

More specifically on the conflict between science and theology, he continues:

> "Science, while conquering them [the theologians], has found in our Scriptures a far nobler truth than that literal historical exactness for which theologians have so long and so vainly contended."[3]

---

1. Stern, *Lichtenberg*, 300.
2. White, *Warfare of Science with Theology*, v–vi.
3. White, *Warfare of Science with Theology*, xii.

xxi

It seems to me that part of the "nobler truth" is not only that *any* relationship can exist between science and religion, but that these two worldviews are even more interrelated today than in the past.

My thesis—and the purpose of this book—is to elaborate on that surprising relationship. One of my first observations of this relationship is between Man's very definition of "self," and Man's discovery of God as a "Higher Self."[4] Most important, in this age of science, we can better understand ancient peoples' belief in a God concerned with their existence, as expressed in the Hebrew Bible. We can see more clearly their perceptions of Time and their views of the Universe as they strive to come closer to that Higher Self.

I believe that White's "nobler truth" is even clearer to us today than it was over a century ago, since scientific study has not only increased our knowledge but also expanded our minds. During the past five hundred years or so, extraordinary thinkers have devised revolutionary methods to explore and analyze the seemingly infinite expanse of space and time, the subquantum level of almost incomprehensibly small matter to include now the "God particle,"[5] and even the virtually invisible process of thought itself. We are thus better able to explain humanity in the natural world today. By extension, we are also better able to understand the thoughts and relationships of people who have inhabited it.

Overview of the Book

In this work, I provide support for my reasoning about the ancient Hebrews' writings and belief in a God concerned for humanity. The Bible that they recorded represents a thousand years of ancient thought, having ended over two millennia ago. Its concept of the "Hebrew Lord"[6] evolves from the primitive in Genesis to the sublime in the books of the prophets. To best explain these perspectives, my discussions of Man, self, God, and the Universe include analyses of Spinoza, Freud, Einstein, and other

---

4. The word "man" has acquired great poetic power over centuries of use in the English language. It is used in this text and by those quoted in its historical sense of referring collectively to all humanity—female and male, child and adult.

5. Editor's note: "God particle" was first coined by Nobel Prize winner Leon Lederman in 1993, then used in 2003 to describe the Higgs-Boson particle—the most elementary particle needed to explain the existence of physical matter.

6. Steiner, "Introduction," in *The Old Testament*, xxiii.

leading thinkers, as well as my own evolving understanding of God in this amazing era of science.

For example, Freud's view of a concerned God was particularly harsh. In writing of religion with his usual panache, he explains:

> The whole thing is so patently infantile, so foreign to reality, that to anyone with a friendly attitude to humanity, it is painful to think that the great majority of mortals will never be able to rise above this view of life. It is still more humiliating to discover how large a number of people living today, who cannot but see that this religion is not tenable, nevertheless try to defend it piece by piece in a series of pitiful rearguard actions.[7]

A great many scholars who pride themselves on their rationality and modernity today concur with Freud. In respectful disagreement, I present reasoning that represents neither wishful thinking nor narrow fundamentalist belief. The science I present is well documented; the biblical translations by authentic scholars are accurate; and I believe my conclusion follows in a natural manner. I ask only that you read with healthy curiosity and an open mind.

Nevertheless, take care not to confuse what I say with spurious beliefs that adherents misleadingly name "Intelligent Design." In their literal biblical interpretations, its proponents claim that the complexities of evolution can only be explained by the existence of a higher being who supposedly guided its development. Their ideas directly clash with Darwin's reasoning and have been shown to be erroneous by countless responsible scientists, time and again.

In contrast, I demonstrate and carefully explicate my reasoning so as to help the reader follow the exposé in each chapter. To set the theme, I end this introduction with a parable to engage the reader in considering the concept of self, more specifically what I call "Personness." In the first chapter, I discuss God's self-definition as found in Exodus and consider it alongside the understanding of self-identity in modern science and philosophy.

In the second chapter, I try to clarify the Hebrew Bible's representation of God, which, in the process of many translations, has repeatedly been misinterpreted. Oxford University don George Steiner, one of academia's leading critics of language, concurs, stating that, "translations from biblical

---

7. Freud, *Civilization and Its Discontents*, 22.

Hebrew are misreadings."[8] I refer instead to original texts based on today's biblical Hebrew scholars' best translations and explanations.

In chapters three and four, I present the views of Baruch Spinoza and Albert Einstein. Spinoza was the first to use scientific knowledge and reasoning in the seventeenth century for the purpose of writing a critique of the Bible. Einstein's twentieth-century understanding of life and the universe was based not only on science but also on Spinoza's philosophy and, perhaps surprisingly to many readers, on the Hebrew Bible as well. Einstein wrote unambiguously that both Spinoza's and his own thinking (in their respective fields) were influenced by their Judaism: "Spinoza's worldview is penetrated by the thought and way of feeling which is so characteristic of the living Jewish intelligence. I feel that I could not be so close to Spinoza were I not myself a Jew, and if I had not developed within a Jewish environment."[9] I discuss this close identification of one Jew to another, despite their separation across three centuries.

The fifth and sixth chapters follow up on Einstein's theories, focusing on aspects of his thought that initiated revolutionary insights into the nature of Time. And I discuss how Einstein's concept of Time (including the self in space-time) was closer to that of the ancient Hebrews than it is to our current, more conventional understanding. Recognizing first that there is a difference in people's concepts of Time, and seeing the fundamental nature of those differences when reading the Bible, are essential to understanding Time, self, and the Bible. For example, I discuss how Einstein's view provides us deeper insight into the ancient Hebrews' thoughts on death (chapter six). This concludes the first section of the book.

The seventh, eighth, and ninth chapters—the heart of the book—provide background and support for Man's evolving relationship with a concerned and evolving God through a study of Samuel Alexander, the first Jew to get a fellowship at Oxford; French Jesuit paleontologist Pierre Teilhard de Chardin, whose work was denounced by the Roman Catholic Church; and Hindu religious scholar Sri Aurobindo, who served under the maharajah in late nineteenth-century India.

8. Steiner, "Introduction," in *The Old Testament*, p. xxiii.

9. Einstein letter to Willy Aron, January 14, 1943, Einstein Archives, Princeton University Press, Princeton, NJ. Commentator (Judith Goldman): Robert Goldman conducted research in the Einstein Archives when they were at the Institute for Advanced Study in Princeton. They are now at the Hebrew University of Jerusalem and available at Einstein Archives Online, Princeton University Press. No archival number could be found for this letter. (Hereafter: Encountered during Robert Goldman's research.)

The final three chapters represent my own reasoning, with evidence and discussion in chapter ten on the Hebrew Lord's relation to the evils of our time, as expressed by Holocaust survivor Elie Wiesel. In the eleventh chapter, I attempt to expound upon the ancient Hebrews' sense of self, in part as defined by H. Wheeler Robinson, who writes about what he calls "corporate personality" in biblical times, and as considered by Etty Hillesum, a young woman who died in Auschwitz. In the final chapter, I look at our place, time, and role in the Universe with a God concerned for Humanity as understood by Plato, Maïmonides, Wittgenstein, Einstein, Gödel, and others.

In these pages, I have tried to write clearly so as to present a rational discussion of philosophers and scientists (some of us are a bit of both) that will bring us closer to understanding the Hebrew Bible's view of reality and God. In a similar attempt at clarity, Rabbi Isaac Cherif, one of the great rabbis of nineteenth-century Lithuania (then an important center of Jewish learning), was interviewing to become rabbi in the city of Slonim. He had the ability to simplify even the most abstruse subjects and to speak so that even a person with the least biblical background would understand. His biblical discourse lasted only twenty-five minutes. Afterwards, the head of the community went to him sorrowfully and said, "I'm afraid you will not be able to serve as our rabbi; everyone in the audience understood what you said!"

I hope to have adequately emulated Rabbi Cherif.

A Parable of Self: Philip's Peril—A Perplexing Property of Personness

It was a dark and stormy night. Philip slogged along a country lane in the dark, the straps of his backpack cutting into his shoulders. He'd laughed off the warning that weather on the English coast this time of year couldn't be trusted. On foot since morning, cold and tired, he'd given up hope of finding the cozy fire and warm bed he'd reserved at the Boar's Head. At this point, any shelter from the drumming rain would do. This last vacation as a bachelor on a solitary walking trip had seemed more exciting a week earlier when he'd told his fiancée, Pam, while sipping French wine in a candlelit Soho restaurant.

He peered ahead in the rain—could that be a cottage with the lights on? He stepped up his pace, and his heart lightened as the shape of an old, ivy-coated country house became clear. As he neared the gate, he saw an overgrown garden surrounding a decrepit structure that he would've thought abandoned, were it not for a flickering lamp seen through a dirt-streaked window. He hesitated, but he was wet and weary; the road ahead promised only darkness, rain, and shrieking wind. So he walked to the door and knocked.

* * *

Philip tugged at knots that clamped his wrists to a chair, but this only caused the rough hemp to press more deeply into his flesh. He tried to move his legs, still in heavy hiking boots, but they, too, were tightly lashed together. Though out of the rain, he thought grimly that his situation had hardly improved.

A mild-mannered, gray-haired man in a white jacket and rimless spectacles entered the room. "Good, you're finally awake," he said to Philip, with a smile, seating himself in a soft, old Morris chair. He leaned back, folded his hands, looked benignly upon his captive, and spoke in the voice of a practiced pedagogue: "Perhaps you'd like to know why you find your-self in this odd position, hm? As you may have surmised, the hot tea you drank contained a fast-acting drug that left you unconscious long enough for me to tie you securely."

He continued, "Let me tell you of myself: I'm a mad scientist, trying to find the nature of the 'self'—that peculiar attribute that tells each person he's himself and not someone else. But where does this feeling of 'person-ness' lie? Is it in the organization of the brain's matter? If so, I hypothesize, an artificially manufactured brain with identical organization should have the same personness, yes? And so we shall see."

Philip stared, incredulous, at the mad scientist, but listened as he con-tinued: "You're a fortunate man, as you're about to play an essential role—that of subject—in an experiment to clarify the problem. Please excuse the manner in which I elicited your involuntary cooperation. We mad scien-tists operate on tight budgets. Funds are scandalously low and my request to hire a replacement research intern was turned down."

Philip gulped, then stuttered, "D-did anything happen to the first?"

"Well," the mad scientist grinned, "it's a trifle embarrassing. You see, I've built a highly sophisticated device for fabricating an exact duplicate of any human body—including the brain—complete with memories, idiosyncrasies, and habits. The technique consists of temporarily stilling life processes by freezing the body, making a frozen copy, then thawing both original and copy."

Philip's jaw dropped open, but the mad scientist continued: "I'd just put your predecessor—a most promising graduate student—in the device and started the process when I got an urgent call. I was to go to London immediately." He changed to a whisper. "They think I'm studying inherited memory in planaria." He cleared his throat. "I left my nurse in charge. She's a lovely girl, but not what you'd call meticulous. She followed my instructions except for one little detail. When she removed the two bodies from the chambers to defrost, she forgot to label the original and the copy. The two were identical; each had the same memories, the same reactions. One's memories, however, were artificial. But which one?"

Philip closed his mouth and began thinking about the admittedly fascinating problem as the mad scientist elaborated. "I'd planned to merely make a copy of the student, which I'd keep for experimentation, then let the young man go back to the university, well compensated for his time. But with no way to tell the original from the copy, well, what could I do? How could the young man prove he was the original?" The mad scientist paused and shook his head sadly at Philip.

He went on. "The original student tried for days to prove he was himself, but the copy did the same thing, and just as well, since it didn't know its memories were fabricated rather than natural. I couldn't tell them apart."

The mad scientist sighed. "Unfortunately, loss of control in the experiment rendered it useless. I spoke strongly to my nurse about the oversight. This question of 'self' is indeed quite a problem. What is this 'you,' this 'self' about which humans are so monomaniacally concerned, but unable to prove to anyone—including themselves—that they are themselves and not a copy?" He paused.

"I'll be more careful with you," the mad scientist added cheerily. "First, I'll put you in the simple duplicating machine, make a copy, labeled in accordance with government regulations as 'Imitation Philip.' You, of course, will be conscious of your own self and body. Imitation Philip will presumably be conscious of itself, too. Then and only then will I exchange brains so your brain is in the copy and the fabricated brain goes to you."

In spite of reassurance about careful control, Philip looked worried. "Oh yes," the mad scientist boasted, "my device can also switch brains! It exchanges each natural cell with its fabricated copy serially, in an ultrahigh-speed, computer-controlled process. When it begins, the frozen brains have a mixture of natural and artificial cells. At any time, I can halt the process, thaw the bodies, wake you both up, and talk to you, if necessary. Hmm." He stared at a blank wall for nearly a minute, then mused to himself, "I wonder where your personness would be at the midpoint?" Philip didn't like the sound of this.

The mad scientist mumbled, again to the wall, "After the brain exchange is complete, your consciousness is in the copy; and a copy consciousness is in your real body. So . . . where, then, are 'you'?"

Again that heavy silence. But the mad man brightened and turned back to face Philip. "Oh well, when I switch brains again—as of course I'll do—your own self will go back to your own body." He paused and closed his eyes. "But what of the self you will have gained while your brain was in the other body? Is it still a part of you even after I take it away? Hmm. I must remember that question!"

"But first," he said softly to Philip, "I'm told that Buddhists believe there is no self. So would any of these switches matter to their concept of personness?" The mad scientist was now speaking very slowly, looking at Philip in the same way he'd been staring blankly at the wall. "At what point in switching brain cells does the feeling of personness leave the body and go into the copy? Since exchanging a cell for an identical one should individually make no difference, what is it that eventually affects your personness? Or if the self doesn't ever move, what determines its stability? Does it matter, for example, that you were in a past location even though you were unconscious? Can self be tied to a former location in space-time? Is the self material? Or intangible? Or . . . ?"

The mad scientist paused and put a hand to his forehead, muttering something about a headache, and reached over to a shelf with two jars of white tablets. Hopefully, the mad scientist, his eyes partly covered by his raised hand, would pick up the bottle of knockout tablets by mistake. Philip watched him pop a pill, draw some water into a beaker, drink, and collapse on the floor.

* * *

Ninety minutes later, Philip was again trudging along the country road in the rain. He'd maneuvered his chair next to a lab bench, picked up a knife with his teeth, and sliced through the ropes. He felt carefree until a disturbing thought struck him: How could he be sure the mad scientist had not already performed the experiment? Perhaps he wasn't himself anymore, but rather only a copy, and the real Philip was still tied up somewhere in the old house. If that were true, what should he do? And would it matter?[10]

10. Editor's note: This is a slightly revised and edited version of Goldman, "Philip's Peril," 131–5.

God's "I" and "I"

Certainly it is correct to say: Conscience is the voice of God.

—Ludwig Wittgenstein[1]

How does God refer to Himself in the Hebrew Bible? Moses asks His name,[2] and in a common English translation, the reply is, "And God said to Moses, 'I am who I am.' He continues, "You shall say this to the children of Israel: 'I AM' sent me to you."[3]

The biblical God may have anticipated the inevitable confusion, so He tries to help, telling Moses how His name relates to humanity—specifically to the Israelites. His brief explanation, "I AM," corresponds to an earlier form of the Hebrew, "He Is." These are words the Israelites understand: the concrete language of ancient Hebrew. The Hebrew Lord says further that He is *not* concrete, not an object, not something that can be described, compared, or imagined. Rather, He is supreme selfness. He simply *is*.[4]

God explains not only that He is "I AM," but He acts through the "I am"—that is, through each individual's consciousness (or "awareness" or "sense") of self. At the same time, "HE IS," indicating that He is a higher

1. Wittgenstein, *Notebooks*, 75e.

2. Exodus 3:13. Commentator: Unless otherwise noted, all translations from the first five books of the Hebrew Bible (the Torah) are from Friedman, *Commentary on the Torah*. Throughout this book, wherever "Lord" is in the translation, the author's preference, "YHWH," is noted in square brackets following: [YHWH].

3. Exodus 3:14. Commentator: Professor Robert J. Littman comments that "To understand the complexity of translating Hebrew, note this explanation: Biblical Hebrew does not have a tense system but rather an aspect system. There is no present, but rather all actions are either completed or incompleted. Hence, when God says 'I am that I am' the incompleted (imperfect) aspect is used. A more accurate but awkward translation would be, 'I was and am and will be what I was and am and will be,' which reflects that God always was and always will be."

4. Cassirer, *Language and Myth*, 76–77.

level of conscience beyond the world of objects (i.e., the objective world). Thus, paradoxically, He is also beyond human conception.

After God identifies Himself in relation to the Israelites and then by His proper name, He describes Himself in the more familiar terms of His relationship to each of the Patriarchs—and thus to each individual self:

> And God said further to Moses, "You shall say this to the children of Israel: 'YHWH, your fathers' God, Abraham's God, Isaac's God, and Jacob's God, has sent me to you.'
> This is my name forever, and this is how I am to be remembered for generation after generation."[5]
> And God spoke to Moses and said to him, "I am YHWH. And I appeared to Abraham, to Isaac, and to Jacob as El Shadday, and I was not known to them by my name, YHWH."[6]

Elsewhere in the Bible, the typical phrasing is, "The God of Abraham, Isaac, and Jacob," not mentioning "The God of" with each name. But in Exodus, God's relationship with each Patriarch is identified, emphasizing the quality of selfness in each man who achieved a higher level of understanding. Individually, they learned to live as their higher selves; collectively, they show us our potential to live as higher selves, too.

This understanding has carried over into the Jewish mystical system of Kabbalah, wherein "It is through a descent into one's own self that a person penetrates the spheres separating Man from God."[7]

French philosopher Gabriel Marcel says that to refer to God in the third person is to fail to comprehend Him. "The being of God," he writes, "holds the 'I' of Man."[8] The Hindu *Upanishad* speaks of finding true enjoyment through the surrender of our individual self to the universal Self.[9] A leading orthodox Jewish scholar, Joseph Soloveitchik, speaks of God as the "Supreme Self."[10] God, then, by such definitions, is not part of the objective world but rather exists on a higher level of selfness than do humans. (Note that the terms "higher" or "deeper" selfness used here are metaphorical,

---

5. Exodus 3:15.

6. Exodus 6:2–3.

7. Ponce, *Kabbalah*, 87.

8. Editor's note: Marcel, *Mystery of Being*.

9. Tagore, *Religion of Man*, 9.

10. Editor's note: Rabbi Joseph Soloveitchik (1903–1993) was an influential Orthodox rabbi and philosopher.

indicating something somehow beyond our own selfness, not physically higher than ourselves, nor physically deeper within us.)

The biblical Hebrews were repeatedly told by God not to try to construct His image, as doing so would encourage thinking of God as an object. Similarly, ancient Jews did not—and religious Jews do not—try to pronounce the name of God. We still do not know how to pronounce God's name. In fact, so many biblical scholars disagree as to whether the phrase "I AM THAT I AM" is accurate that the Jewish Publication Society's 1985 biblical translation avoids the issue altogether: it simply keeps the Hebrew transliteration: Ehyeh-Asher-Ehyeh.[11]

God's Name in Mistranslation

The nuances and multiple meanings of God's responses about His identity are lost in English biblical translations, which usually replace the name of God from the Hebrew text simply with "The Lord."[12] This is actually a mistranslation—or a lack of translation, accompanied by a euphemism. It offers the modern reader no inkling of the radical change in thought that ancient Israelites had to experience: to go from considering the concept of God iconically, as did the Baal worshippers and Egyptians (i.e., represented by stone statues), to instead thinking of God abstractly, as the Supreme or Higher Self, only knowable by achieving a higher level of inner awareness of their own lesser selves.

This distinction requires a different way of thinking about theological matters, both in ancient times and today.

God as the Higher Self

Consider, for example, prayer. In the Hebrew tradition, true prayer is not worshipping an entity and asking for something or for some desire to be

---

11. Exodus 3:14. Jewish Publication Society, *Tanakh*, 88.

12. Whenever God's name YHWH appears, the word "Adonai" is read by observant Jews. There was a prohibition about saying the name of God aloud, except by the high priest on Yom Kippur. Adonai is translated as "Lord," and hence in many English translations, God's name does not appear. "Jehovah" is another euphemism for YHWH. This is a deliberate mixing of the vowels of Adonai with the consonants of YHVH so as not to pronounce the name of God. (The author credits Professor Robert J. Littman for this information.)

fulfilled. If there is a God, He exists on a higher level of reality than our own. And if God is this Higher Self, we cannot seek Him on a literal level, since He has no physical presence, as would a statue or a charm. Therefore, we can only try to reach Him by acting in a way that we believe would satisfy Him enough to relate to us: this includes our prayers. A person who prays is opening and making bare his inner self (some would say "soul") so that the Higher Selfness, which transcends his own, can enter, touching and affecting his thought and action.

God Seeks Man

However, as the Hebrew Bible tells us again and again, it is difficult for humans to act in a manner to which God relates, and it is a very complicated thing for man to be able to find God, because God is this "Higher Self." But God, who seeks to act through man, asks that we take action in a way aspiring to higher qualities, to the Higher Self not through isolated reflection but through action in the world.

Scientific progress is one kind of action that helps man move toward a higher understanding of self. It is the responsibility of man to continue to take such actions, so as to engender the relationship not only that man seeks with God but that God also wants with man.

Biblical scholar Abraham Joshua Heschel[13] explains that God also is in search of man: "The primary type of biblical thinking is not man's knowledge of God but man's being known by God. Man's awareness of God is awareness of God not as an object of thinking but as a subject. Awareness of God is awareness of being thought of by God, of being an object of his concern, of his expectation."[14]

So how do we contribute to this knowing? One way is to act uprightly in the manner God decrees. For example, according to Emmanuel Levinas,[15] you find God in the face of the person who needs you, your help, or your love. In meeting that need, you experience closeness to God, who acts through your selfness—that is, through your conscience and your will. Another method is to act in such a way as to attract God's mercy:

13. Heschel taught at the Jewish Theological Seminary in New York.

14. Heschel, *Moral Grandeur and Spiritual Audacity*, 373.

15. Levinas was a leading existentialist philosopher and Talmudic scholar who taught at the Sorbonne in Paris until his death in 1995.

It is . . . why in so many psalms the speaker goes on at great length about his own lowly state, frequently identifying himself as poor, downtrodden, or oppressed. Apparently, it is only necessary to arouse God's natural pity.[16]

. . .

Even kings, when they approach God in the Bible, are said to be downtrodden and oppressed, since that is the condition most likely to bring a response from God.[17]

But how can we know if there truly is a greater Self that enters our own? How can we know if a higher and deeper Selfness is shared with others? That is, how can we know if that which we call "God" and the ancient Hebrews called YHWH even exists?

Moreover, if there is such a fuller self-consciousness capable of penetrating our own, why believe it to be beneficial to humanity?

Understanding Selfness

In my attempt to answer these questions, I start first with the existence of self. As I demonstrate in the parable "Philip's Peril" (see introduction), there is something of which we are aware, beyond our corporeal being, beyond our unique gene makeup; we call it "self." It is that intangible quality that makes each person unique, though science has not yet isolated the physical or chemical properties that define it.

Thus, the biblical identification of God with higher selfness is intriguing; the concept of self that was mystery back then seems to remain mystery now. The location of "selfness" has eluded modern science, and perhaps "Higher Selfness" is destined to be the same mystery. But before abandoning it to the realm of the incomprehensible, first allow me to take you through the next parable, this time to consider the concept of "object selfness" next to "human selfness."

16. Kugel, *The God of Old*, 56.
17. Kugel, *The God of Old*, 59.

Another Parable of Self

Would you be you, if you were conceived of the same parents but a month earlier of later?[18] That person would have innate characteristics different from yours, but would that person be you with the same feeling of self that you possess? That person would be able to feel joy and pain, but would it be you feeling that joy and pain? The question is not nonsensical—and in some far future time, it may even be of practical importance. Consider the question in my adaptation of the following ancient story.

The Ship of Theseus and the Self

In Athens, a ship built of wooden planks is put in dry dock. It is called the ship of Theseus, because it is said to have carried him home from victory over the Minotaur. The Athenians wished to preserve the ship, so one by one, each plank was removed and replaced by one newly cut. The ship remains otherwise whole throughout the arduous process.

However, the removed planks are not destroyed but used, rather, to build another ship identical to the original.

When the process is complete, which one of the ships is that of Theseus?

Is it the first one—that, though made of new timber, has in the gradual procedure never changed its identity? Or is it the second ship—that, though newly built, consists of the original lumber? If you believe it to be the second, at what point did the identity of the ship of Theseus jump from one to the other?

Now, instead of inanimate ships, imagine we were talking about live humans. Which person would be the true self from before such surgery? Consider further if you had undergone this procedure in a tyrant-controlled nation and had been told that before surgery, only one of the two resulting beings would be allowed to live. Whom should it be?

If you think the survivor is the second person, made of parts removed from your original body, then you assume that physical parts make up your whole, which includes your self. Since "self" is not a body part that was transferred, when did your true self jump into the second body from the one in which you started?

18. This use of the word "you" is technically wrong, since the person indicated here as "you" may not be—but you get the idea.

If you choose the first person to survive, you are assuming a continuity of sense of self that does not depend on physical components; instead, unique selfness is found in the original arrangement of parts, not in the parts themselves.

For either choice, the "self"—that which underlies the statement "I am"—is fundamentally material being. This leads back to the ancient Hebrew understanding that the Higher Self—God—is also noncorporeal and thus cannot be embodied in an object (as previous religions had represented their gods).[19]

Of Science, Self, and Consciousness

Perhaps someday, science will be able to explain how the feeling of selfness arises and what it is to be conscious of this self. However, as many specialists in the field of cognitive studies claim, the phenomenon of self-consciousness will always be a mystery.

While grasping the concept of "self" is complex, it is a prerequisite for understanding "self-consciousness." Another requirement is getting a handle on the notion of "consciousness" itself. Scientists and philosophers alike have struggled with this conundrum for ages, so here I shall examine some of their best efforts.

I once had the opportunity in Princeton to ask Albert Einstein's close friend, the logician Kurt Gödel, about a note Einstein wrote discussing consciousness. Gödel told me Einstein believed that science could never explain consciousness, that "the methods of science lead away from the life-world."[20]

Looking instead to philosophy for an answer to the problem of consciousness, there still remains the difficulty of defining, identifying, and reducing it to its basic components. John Searle explains:

> Consciousness is not reducible in the way that other biological properties typically are. . . . Consciousness only exists when it is experienced as such. For other features, such as growth, digestion, and photosynthesis, you can make a distinction between our experience of the feature, and the feature itself. This possibility makes reduction of those other features possible. But you cannot make

19. Plutarch, *Life of Theseus,* written about 100 CE. In Plutarch's telling, the second ship is not built.

20. I spoke with Gödel on August 14, 1977. See chapter twelve.

the reduction for consciousness without losing the point of having the concept in the first place. Consciousness and the experience of consciousness are the same thing.[21]

This still does not adequately illuminate us on the topic, but as we go to another leading philosopher of the mind, Colin McGinn, we begin to sense a potential futility of the chase to understand; he states that due to the limitations of the human brain, consciousness will always be beyond our understanding.[22] Nevertheless, most physicists and biologists say—and I agree—that consciousness emerges from the active interrelation of neurons and other components in the brain. Yet the manner of this interaction is still unknown.

One popular attempt at explanation has been that consciousness relates to the brain in the way that computer software (i.e., the program) relates to computer hardware (i.e., the physical equipment). But I believe this to be too crude an analogy. At best, it shows that reality need not be material. A program is real—the computer would be useless junk without it—but the program itself is not material, though it can be manifested in different ways or in different substances.

It seems that even simple questions of consciousness remain beyond our ken. Engineers build computers with programs that can answer questions in a specific field with what appear to be intelligent replies. And it is clear that computer programs are being written that can respond with seeming intelligence in any area of human knowledge. But is such a computer (or its program) conscious?

We do have a way—though not foolproof—for determining whether or not a computer is conscious. It was proposed in the early days of digital computers by the illustrious pioneer Alan Turing.[23] An intelligent person and the computer being tested are located separately where the person inquiring cannot see either human or computer. All participants communicate by keyboard. The inquirer asks questions of the human subject and of the computer, not knowing which is human.

The inquirer cannot ask questions concerning the "self" of the addressee (e.g., "Are you conscious?"), because both person and computer will reply "yes." If, after lengthy questioning, the inquirer cannot determine

---

21. Searle, *Mystery of Consciousness*, 213-4. See also Bermudez, *Paradox of Consciousness*.

22. McGinn, *The Mysterious Flame*, 214.

23. Now known as the "Turing test."

which is the person, the computer is said to have passed the test for consciousness. Although no computer has yet passed the Turing test, some have nearly done so.[24] Unfortunately, however, this exercise still does not enlighten us as to the nature of consciousness. And the question of "self-consciousness" is just as elusive.

Furthermore, what are the boundaries of self? Eric B. Baum tells of an experiment devised by V. S. Ramachandran[25] to try and define those boundaries:

> Hold your hand under the table where you can't see it, and have a confederate stroke your hand below the table at the same exact times she strokes the table in your sight. Rapidly, you develop the sensation that the table is part of yourself. This sensation is deeply held, as can be demonstrated by wiring yourself up to measure your galvanic skin response. The galvanic skin response is not under conscious control but rises in response to stress. Now, once you are wired up, and the stroking is going on so that you think the table is part of you, have a confederate surprise you by smashing the table with a hammer. You flinch, and your galvanic skin response skyrockets, as it would if you saw someone smashing your hand with a hammer. This galvanic skin response is not produced if someone smashes the table without first achieving the sense of self in the table through simultaneous stroking of the table and the hand.[26]

Note: If you decide to perform this experiment, it is probably not a good idea to use a table cherished by friend or family.

But the exercise does achieve the effect of blurring the boundaries of the human self. More important, it demonstrates the plasticity of the self in its ability to relate to other selves—even to inanimate objects. Yet it still does not facilitate our efforts to define either those boundaries or the self they actually surround.

---

24. Editor's note: Recent competitions have invited challenges to the Turing test (e.g., Elbot, the software program created by Fred Roberts in 2008, and Watson, the IBM supercomputer that beat a human contestant in 2011 at *Jeopardy*, showed superb linguistic understanding and manipulation). Several computer programs have been judged to succeed, but critics dispute their success. The question of the nature of consciousness has yet to be answered.

25. A neuroscientist known primarily for his work in the fields of behavioral neurology and visual psychophysics.

26. Baum, *What Is Thought?* 406.

It appears, then, that today's science is still unable to satisfactorily explain "selfness." However, in the Hebrew Bible, as noted earlier, God had Moses tell the people His name, "I AM," meaning "Supreme Selfness." (In biblical usage, a proper noun often described the qualities of its possessor.) The Bible also recounts stories of men and women who speak of their own sense of self, with the chance to say, simply, "I am." In this way, both God and man—that is, "Higher Self" and "lesser self"—find a means of relating to each other.

And although science has yet to satisfactorily define either term, scientific research (done by humans, of course) contributes to advances in man's personal development of self. Much of this research has been done with computers, as I discuss in the next chapter.

What Is Man?

What is man that You have been mindful of him,
mortal man that You have taken note of him,
that You have made him little less than divine,
and adorned him with glory and majesty.

—Psalm 8:4–6

2

Biblical Meaning: Lost in Translation

Reading the Bible in translation is like kissing
the girl you love through a veil.

—CHAIM NACHMAN BIALIK[1]

IN THE MID-TWENTIETH CENTURY, computers were erratic, room-filling behemoths, stupefyingly slow and limited in capability compared to today's models. At the time, however, the machines did not seem so primitive. Enthusiastic engineers, programmers, and promoters made extravagant claims for computers, though each had a small fraction of the power contained in today's dollar-store graphing calculator.

One particularly interesting claim, however, was that the computer could translate texts between languages. Naturally, the United States Department of Defense was interested. Automatic translation between Russian and English would greatly simplify gathering strategic military intelligence, for example. The government generously poured funds into computerized translation research.

Early on, researchers proudly announced that they were well on the way, having succeeded in translating from one language to another, using tiny vocabularies and simplified grammar. Embarrassingly, though, they could not get much further. Human intervention was still needed for meaningful translations.

In 1960, a leading researcher in mechanical translation, Yehoshua Bar-Hillel,[2] explained why. To accurately translate a text, he affirmed, a computer program would need to *implicitly* understand the world to which

1. Chaim Nachman Bialik, 1873–1934, was a Jewish poet, quoted frequently without reference.

2. Bar-Hillel, "Present Status," 91–163.

the text refers. This understanding would require not only great perspicacity but also extensive computer programming capacity. Additionally, the programmer would need superb knowledge of context, along with empathetic and cultural understanding.

This standard illustrates why biblical translations from ancient Hebrew cannot possibly be reliable. Bible translators would need such qualities to be true to the original intent of the text. In reaching back to a long-ago society so different from our own on most levels, today's translators, by definition, lack sufficient contextual understanding of the era, empathy, and general common ground to reframe that ancient society into a different language.

In fact, most linguists would say that any translation necessarily loses many rich qualities of the original text, as language conveys much more than grammatical elements that refer to common objects or activity. Even in simple words such as "play" or "work," which seem to translate easily, there are potentially countless different interpretations at the cultural, racial, social, economic, sexual, humorous, spiritual, and other levels of understanding. Yet in order to share even the general ideas of those from different eras or countries, we must make do with the best translations available. And for now, the best ones are still those done by humans—even with all the shortcomings mentioned earlier.

Lost Understanding, Lost Meaning

Unfortunately, much of the deep spirituality of the Hebrew Bible is missing in currently available English translations. Biblical Hebrew was spoken by an ancient people with a different understanding of reality from that which we have nowadays, thousands of years later. In English translation, its compact beauty of expression is gone, its ideas misinterpreted, its underlying meaning distorted.

The Hebrew Bible was written down over a period of centuries. The early translation into Greek was in the second century BCE, when many Jews were living in a society dominated by Greek culture and spiritual beliefs. Similarly, in modern times Jews have coexisted in a culturally Christian world, absorbing a view of spirituality derived from that influence as well.

Many Jewish sects emerged from ancient times, though two of these dominated: the *Pharisees*, influenced by Hellenistic (Greek) thought, and the *Sadducees*, who adhered more literally to the Hebrew Bible. But the

Pharisee-Saducee controversy emerged only several centuries later, when it is believed the Hebrew Bible was completed.

Translations from the original text into Greek and eventually into English led to a number of fundamental misunderstandings. For example, the Hebrew word "*nefesh*" was translated as "soul" in the English Bible, although a more accurate translation would be "self." It is this original "self"—with all the mystery it implies—through which much Jewish spirituality is sought. *Nefesh* is the seat of physical breathing, conscious life, and emotional states such as anxiety, grief, and joy. In the fullness of living, therefore, Jewish spirituality means being involved in the world and in the lives of others.

The Talmud and today's Judaism grew out of *Pharisaism*.[3] In this belief, a human being was thought to be made up of a material body and a spiritual soul. Yet ancient Hebrew had no word corresponding to the Greek "psyche" or to the English language "soul."

Consequently, I believe that the true spirituality of the original text has been lost.

To an ancient Hebrew, the world itself was infused with spirituality *within* the presence of God—not divided between the material and the spiritual, as became the Christian view. This is illustrated in the following figure by John Shelby Spong:[4]

---

3. In the religiously tumultuous times of two thousand years ago, there were many cults in both the Jewish and non-Jewish world. When Paul, the father of Christian theology, preached between about 40 and 70 CE, the *Pharisees* and *Sadducees* were the major Jewish sects. It is generally believed that Jesus was a Pharisee.

4. Spong, *Hebrew Lord*, 34, 40. Spong is the retired bishop of the Diocese of Newark, New Jersey. In referring to his book, it is important to note that the "Hebrew Lord" of the title is not God, but Jesus.

Contrast between Hebrew and Christian Worldviews

THE HEBREW VIEW

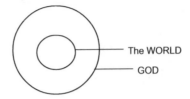

The WORLD

GOD

THE CHRISTIAN VIEW

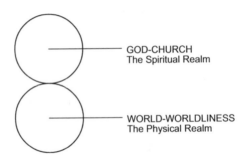

GOD-CHURCH
The Spiritual Realm

WORLD-WORLDLINESS
The Physical Realm

Further evidence of the loss of original meaning and intent comes from Episcopalian scholar Bishop John Shelby Spong, who contrasted contemporary Christian belief with original Hebrew meanings when he wrote for his Christian readers that "spiritual" is defined as "our traditional [Christian] language has come to think of it: pious, detached, given to contemplation, life-denying, and otherworldly." As for ancient Jews, he continues, "In a Hebrew or biblical context, to be spiritual was to be animated, vital, alive physically, which is quite different from its traditional [Christian] religious meaning."[5]

Bishop Spong provides further differences on the topic of faith: "What we cannot understand, religious [Christian] people assure us, we must accept on faith, with a mighty effort of repression of whatever makes believing difficult. . . . Religiously [in Christianity], to have faith is to believe properly, without doubt." In contrast, Jews believed that, "Biblically,

5. Spong, *Hebrew Lord*, 18, 19.

to have faith is to enter life with the courageous expectation that the more deeply one lives, the more deeply one will experience the God who is revealed in life."[6] The bishop cites the establishment of Israel after two thousand years of Jewish homelessness without loss of identity as a contemporary example of such biblical faith.

Spong also contrasts Christian and Jewish meanings[7] of "salvation": "Salvation, in its traditional [Christian] religious definition, means 'being saved; guaranteed heaven; the event beyond life.' Biblically, salvation means 'the fullness of living now as well as eternally.' Eternity has little reality for the Hebrew, except insofar as it was received in the *now* of their lives."[8]

Such vastly different cultural interpretations are both the cause and effect of translating a text into other languages. The case of "salvation," for example, reveals a fundamental truth about the Hebrew sense of self; Jews cannot depend upon an afterlife to find the comfort or fulfillment of salvation. Rather, they must actively strive to achieve it within their own lifetimes—through study, good deeds, and living a shared past, present, and future under God— that is, living *olam*.[9] It is therefore worth looking at biblical translations in terms of Jewish identity and man's relationship with God.

First Bible Translations

The Hebrew Bible was first translated into another tongue about 2,300 years ago in Egypt. Alexandria, one of the great cities of the ancient world, had a large Jewish population that spoke the local language—in this case, Greek. So the Bible was translated into Greek, not only for Jews who no longer understood Hebrew but also (later) for Christians who wished to comment on and criticize the Bible. At the time, in fact, most Jews both in and out of the land of Israel no longer spoke Hebrew as an everyday language either. The common people spoke Aramaic and the upper classes spoke Greek.

6. Spong, *Hebrew Lord*, 22, 23.

7. Editor's note: It seems that Spong's criticism of Christianity is tied, in no small part, to Hebrew mistranslations into Greek and English, which have been acknowledged as such by many biblical scholars. However, he himself remains a highly controversial figure, and the mistakes have not generally been corrected—perhaps because the new versus intended meanings are consistent with Christian theology.

8. Spong, *Hebrew Lord*, 29.

9. Editor's note: The concept of *olam* is discussed in greater depth in chapters 6, 10, 11, 12, and the afterword.

Early rabbis lamented biblical translations into Greek for distorting the intended, original message of the Bible. It is even written in the Talmud that the day the Bible was translated into Greek was as harmful to Israel as the day the golden calf was made.[10]

Centuries later, Martin Luther (certainly no friend of the Jews) wrote, "If I were younger, I would want to learn this language [Hebrew], because no one can really understand the Scriptures without it. For although the New Testament is written in Greek, it is full of Hebraisms and Hebrew expressions. It has therefore been aptly said that the Hebrews drink from the spring, the Greeks from the stream that flows from it, and the Latins from a downstream pool."[11]

Today, biblical translations from the Hebrew are still often deplored. Oxford University's George Steiner bluntly calls them "misreadings." He says that they are even worse than translations "from the most remote and difficult poetry or philosophy."[12] As one of today's foremost critics of language, Steiner wrote this devastating comment in his introduction to a new English edition of the Bible. Publishers of English translations may not have appreciated it.

Further, Nietzsche (author of the infamous line, "God is dead") also spoke of the failed translations following the original Hebrew Bible: "The Jewish Old Testament—the book of divine justice—portrays people, things, and utterances in such a grand style that nothing in Greek or Indian writing can be compared to it. With fear and admiration, we stand in the presence of these tremendous remnants of what man used to be."[13]

Trashing the Hebrew Bible

Yet it is not only bad translation that is at fault in misinterpretations of the Hebrew Bible. Religious bias plays a role, too. Political strategists claim, and events unfortunately demonstrate, that if you tell a lie often enough and in different ways, people will eventually believe it. This technique has long been used against the Hebrew Bible.

In 397 CE, the Christian order of the biblical books, including the Hebrew ones, was specified, after much controversy, by the Catholic

10. Talmud, *Sofrim* I, 7.

11. Wilson, *Our Father Abraham*, 136–7.

12. Steiner, "Introduction," in *The Old Testament*, xxiii.

13. Nietzsche, *Beyond Good and Evil*, Section 52.

Council of Carthage.[14] Since then, the Hebrew Bible has been given bad press in the Christian world. Even the name generally given to it is demeaning, implying that it has been surpassed—"Old Testament" as contrasted with the "New."

The Hebrew Bible (which I differentiate from the Christian "Old Testament") is divided into three parts. The first, consisting of Genesis, Exodus, Leviticus, Numbers, and Deuteronomy, is called "The Five Books of Moses" and is often referred to as "The Torah." The second, called "Prophets," consists of earlier historical books and words by the prophets. The third, "Writings," includes the remaining biblical books. The last book of the Hebrew Bible, "Second Chronicles," concludes with the King of Persia's proclamation permitting the Jews to return from exile in Babylon: "Thus said King Cyrus of Persia: 'THE LORD [YHWH], God of Heaven, has given me all the kingdoms of the earth, and he charged me with building Him a House in Jerusalem, which is in Judah. Any one of you of all His people, the Lord [YHWH] his God be with him and let him go up!'"[15]

The Catholic Council did not find such an "upbeat" ending of the Hebrew Bible to their liking, so they simply changed the order of the books. In defiance of chronology, they put the prophets at the end, so that their "Old Testament" would conclude with Malachi. Christians then reinterpreted the conclusion to foretell the coming of Jesus. Their "Old Testament" now ended, "lest I come and smite the land with a curse."[16]

Many bookstores today contain a confusingly huge number of different translations of the Christian Bible, but in one respect they are all alike: the portion called the "Old Testament" ends with these same words: "smite the land with a curse."

So, for almost two millennia, Christian theologians have claimed that the "New Testament" supersedes the Hebrew Bible, because it replaces the rule of law with that of love.

However, Christians seem to have forgotten that Jesus did not know the New Testament; he was a Jew who had read the Hebrew Bible, including the ancient book of Leviticus in which the golden rule is found: "And

---

14. Carthage was then a Roman colony. In 146 BCE, the Roman army destroyed the original Carthage, founded by the Phoenicians.

15. II Chronicles 36:23.

16. Malachi 4:6. Lockman Foundation, *New American Standard Bible.* Hereafter NASB.

you shall love your neighbor as yourself. I am YHWH,"[17] a text written hundreds of years before it was ever adopted in the New Testament. Furthermore, it is in the Hebrew Bible's book of Deuteronomy that we read the strongest statement for the love of God. In Moses' words,

> And you shall love YHWH, your God, with all your heart, all your soul, and all your might.
> And these words I command you today shall be on your heart.
> And you shall impart them to your children, and you shall speak about them when you sit in your house and when you go in the road and when you lie down and when you get up.
> And you shall bind them for a sign on your hand, and they shall become bands between your eyes.
> And you shall write them on the doorposts of your house and in your gates.[18]

Thus it is evident that the Hebrew Bible strives to build a social order and family structure equitable for its time. In contrast, passages in the New Testament seem to destroy, or at least deny the importance, of such loving familial structures for the living.[19] According to the gospel of Luke: "And Peter said, 'Behold, we have left our own homes, and followed you.' And he [Jesus] said to them, 'Truly I say to you, there is no one who has left house or wife or brothers or parents or children, for the sake of the Kingdom of God, who will not receive many times as much at this time and in the age to come, eternal life.'"[20]

Here the New Testament appears to be promoting a salvation that willingly disregards others, *including one's own family*. Christian theologians believed that virtue was required to receive a reward (salvation), but such a quid pro quo seems not truly virtuous. They also criticize Hebrew scripture for saying nothing about salvation after death—a lack, they argue, that is fortunately rectified in the New Testament.

But what happened to "Love," when a love for God does not necessarily include love for each other? By failing to understand the original Hebrew Bible, Christian critics have also failed to interpret and to translate

---

17. Leviticus 19:18. Friedman, *Commentary on the Torah*.

18. Deuteronomy 6:5–9.

19. An excellent analysis of these matters is found in Kaufmann, *Faith of a Heretic*, 219–29. Kaufmann was professor of philosophy at Princeton.

20. Luke 18.28–30. NASB.

accurately the ancient Hebrew view of life. But they have identified differences between the Hebrew Bible and the New Testament.

Different Views of Life

Jews and Christians do have fundamentally different understandings of life. Some of these have been expressed by Russian Orthodox author Leo Tolstoy, who devoted himself later in life to intense religious study for eight years, after writing the great novels, *War and Peace* and *Anna Karenina*. As a middle-aged man, he studied with a rabbi, and upon great reflection he contrasted Christianity and Judaism in this way:

> The chief distinction between our understanding of human life and that of the Jews consists in this, that according to our understanding our mortal life, transmitted from generation to generation, is not real life but a fallen life, for some reason temporarily spoiled; but in the Jewish conception this life is the most real, it is the highest good, given to man on condition that he fulfills the will of God. From our point of view, the transmission of that fallen life from generation to generation is the continuation of a curse. From the point of view of the Jews, it is the highest blessing attainable by man and to be reached only by fulfilling God's will.[21]

Noted biblical scholar and Jesuit John L. McKenzie adds the importance to Jews of living real life in a way connected to God: "To the Hebrew, life was more than animal vitality, more than human activity and energy; life was association with the Lord, who not only dwelt among His people, but joined Himself to each one of His people who sought Him. In possessing Him was a satisfaction greater than anything which mere human endeavor could obtain."[22]

In other words, Judaism emphasized the nature of the moral life one leads as being of primary religious value. This notion has survived from the time of the ancient prophets until today:

> . . . this is the fast I desire:
> To unlock fetters of wickedness,
> And untie the cords of the yoke.
> To let the oppressed go free;

21. Tolstoy, *A Confession*, 441.
22. McKenzie, *The Two-Edged Sword*, 287.

To break off every yoke.

It is to share your bread with the hungry,

And to take the wretched poor into your home;

When you see the naked, to clothe him,

And not to ignore your own kin.[23]

French existentialist and Talmudic scholar Emmanuel Levinas concurs, commenting on Isaiah 58: "Certainly no religion excludes the ethical. Each one invokes it, but tends also to place what is specifically religious above it, and does not hesitate to 'liberate' the religious from moral obligations. Think of Kierkegaard. On the other hand, what we are told by the rest of this prophetic text is that the religious is at its zenith in the ethical movement towards the other person; that the very proximity of God is inseparable from the ethical transformation of the social."[24]

In other words, it is impossible to distinguish the relationship of God in a person's daily life from people's ethical behavior towards each other; they are inextricably linked. This interpretation of the Hebrew Bible from Jewish philosopher Levinas is perhaps not surprising, but it aligns with that of the Episcopalian Spong and the Russian Orthodox Tolstoy. Such a cross-cultural understanding of the Hebrew Lord demonstrates an understanding of the ancient Hebrews.

The present discussion is intended to further clarify the role of the Hebrew Lord today—in an age of science—by inquiring into the nature of time itself.

The Ancient Hebrew Sense of Time

In today's Western world, when we think of time, we see ourselves as living in the present, marching ahead into an unknown future, with a completed past behind us, so that only the present remains "real." The future does not yet exist; the past no longer does. But ancient Hebrews saw time quite differently.

The nature of the ancient Hebrew language, the way Hebrew prophets spoke about the past and future, and the interpretation of past events suggest that in the biblical mind, past and future events are all alive.

23. Isaiah 58:6–7. JPS.

24. Levinas, *Beyond the Verse*, 5.

Linguistic analyses of written, prophesied events described by ancient Hebrews support this idea. Though we cannot put ourselves entirely in the minds of those who recorded the Bible so many centuries ago, we can examine the concept of time from Einstein's perspective, which, surprisingly, has many similarities to the understanding of time expressed by ancient Hebrews.

Take first, biblical Hebrew itself, which has no past, present, or future tense, unlike most languages. Instead it has two aspects: one for finished and another for unfinished actions. Now consider a prophesied event. In Hebrew, it would *not* be described as an event not yet having happened, but rather as an *existing* event that is either complete or not. George Steiner explains this subtle difference in this way: "In one sense, the foretold has already been accomplished. . . . In another it is eternally present."[25] In either case, there is a sense that the future already exists in the present, or the present in the past.

To illustrate, imagine that the ancients viewed time as would a rower in a rowboat on the water. In such a position, they would literally be facing the past, which would be spread out clearly before their eyes. The future, however, would be out of sight, "behind" them, though they would be moving towards it.

Also supporting this notion that the past is part of the present and future is a linguistic finding by J. N. Schofield of Cambridge University, who discovered that the ancient Hebrew words for "the early days," "the former times," and "what happened before" actually mean "what is in front, or faced."[26] It clearly made sense to the ancients that the past was real, visible in their present, and that past patterns would exist in the future.

Biblical language has a sense of intense immediacy, be it past, present, or future. For example, William Saulez describes a text in which an ancient Hebrew "threw himself either backward or forward into the scene he describes, as if he himself were part of the scene."[27]

This flexibility in time perception is actually not far afield from Einstein's special theory of relativity, as integrated into Rakic's "Open Future View."[28] Rakic found that the past and present are real, and though the

---

25. Steiner, "Introduction," in *The Old Testament*, xxiii.

26. Schofield, *Introducing Old Testament Theology*, 27.

27. Saulez, *Romance of the Hebrew Language*, 107–9. Saulez credits G. R. Driver for his understanding.

28. Editor's note: Nataša Rakic, "Past, Present, Future," 257–80.

future is not yet reality, it could easily be added to Einstein's four-dimensional space-time (axes x, y, and z in three-dimensional space, with the fourth being time itself).

The ancient Hebrews' acceptance as "real" all three tenses of time (past, present, and future) thus places them in much the same belief system as quantum physicists: time is a matter of perspective and must be considered on the space-time continuum.

Conversely, we as Americans and westerners today tend to consider time an objective reality, only thinking of the present as real (because, as the argument goes, the past is gone and the future is unknown). But Einstein determined that there simply is no objective reality regarding space or time. Writer Lincoln Barnett reiterated Einstein's words for the layman: "Time has no independent existence, apart from the order of events by which we measure it."[29]

Yet we persist in seeing time as an objective measurement to which we are held accountable for practical purposes—to arrive at work or school at an appointed hour, to catch the 6:57 a.m. bus, to count down the timer for a four-minute egg, to match the beat of a metronome, and so on. As Klaus Riegel explains, today we experience time as periodicity, which we learn through periodic changes of the seasons, days, moments of hunger, thirst, fatigue, and other identifiable units.[30]

One question that persists about periodicity, though, is whether it is naturally occurring and exists "out there," independent of who experiences it. If not, and if periodicity is instead uniquely "derived" from experience as Riegel says, our understanding of time may be closer to Einstein's special theory of relativity, in which space-time is "perceived" differently by each observer and can change with each new experience.

Greek scientists "rarely viewed time as a continuous dimension." There is evidence, however, that ancient Hebrews did have a kind of understanding of space-time as a continuum.[31] Perhaps this knowledge was lost because it had no immediate applicability, or maybe it was literally lost in translation. In any case, it fortunately was rediscovered by Albert Einstein, more than three thousand years later.

---

29. Editor's note: Barnett, *Universe and Dr. Einstein*, 19. Einstein approved the manuscript and even wrote the foreword to Barnett's book, trying to make relativity more accessible to the layman.

30. Editor's note: Cited in Riegel, "Time and Change," 81–113.

31. Riegel, "Time and Change," 84.

Remembrance as an Active Experience

The Hebrew word for "remember," *zakhor*, means more than its common English translation. Biblical scholar Brevard S. Childs writes, "The act of remembrance is not a simple inner reflection, but involves an action, an encounter with historical events."[32]

Biblical remembrance is an emotional and multisensory experience that puts the Self into a living past. Many Jews feel some of this during the Passover seder. The story of Exodus in the Bible reads, "Remember this day in which you went out from Egypt, from a house of slaves."[33] Participants respond during the seder by eating matzoh and other symbolic foods while reading the *Haggadah*—essentially putting themselves into the story and experiencing it through all the senses in what amounts to a personal encounter with the past.

Notably, in the Hebrew Bible, *zakhor* is usually used in sentences with God or Israel as the subject.[34] The implication seems to be that both God and the people of Israel must actively remember their history—and do so together. But *zakhor*'s spiritual import is often lost when translated.

For example, a psalm in the Jewish Publication Society's Bible translation has a speaker say to God, "Your fame endures throughout the ages."[35] The word translated as "fame" is actually the noun form of *zakhor*, meaning remembrance in the form of a personal encounter with history, as discussed above. The phrase translated "throughout the ages" literally means in Hebrew, "generation to generation." I believe a more insightful interpretation of that line would be, "You are personally encountered in every generation," because it communicates the same, firm religious assertion found in the original Hebrew.

The Jewish Publication Society's English translation referring to "fame," on the other hand, implies no emotional connection and refers merely to a widespread or well-known phenomenon. The result is a bland, innocuous statement devoid of its original depth of meaning that ignores altogether the participative element of "remembrance"—so essential to the Jewish spirit.

---

32. Childs, *Memory and Tradition in Israel*, 88.
33. Exodus 13:3. Friedman, *Commentary on the Torah*.
34. Yerushalmi, *Zakhor*, 5.
35. Psalm 102:13. JPS.

Again and again in the Bible, God exhorts Israel to remember His name, "I AM,"—as frequently expressed in the intense grammatical form of *zakhor*. To better comprehend that appeal, recall the biblical meaning of God's name discussed earlier: One who acts through the self-consciousness of man, and as a Supreme Self, existing beyond the human form of "I am." But if remembrance of this is of utmost importance, it generally is not adequately expressed.

This, too, seems to have been lost in translation.

A Relationship with God in Life

Biblical words relating to the concept of "self" carry richer meaning than do their English counterparts. This is true for many words translated from ancient Hebrew—and probably from other ancient languages as well. In fact, the act of translation is actually a delicate art for which one needs a thorough cultural and linguistic background in the target language, as the contextual meaning of the original word might require an entire phrase in translation to most accurately convey its sense.

Consider the word "*shalom*," so familiar today, for example. It is translated as "peace." But its biblical meaning refers also to a wholeness, a feeling of well-being in the fullness of life. In fact, a contemporary biblical scholar who has studied the term in depth says that shalom is the gift of God that one experiences in the presence of God.[36] Such spiritual meaning in the Hebrew Bible is sought and understood in the context of biblical time, in which past events continue to be real and future events are already accomplished.

Likewise, ancient Hebrew spirituality is not an escape from a physical world or everyday life, as it is in normative Christian beliefs that separate body from soul and matter from spirit. Instead, spirituality for the ancient Hebrew is an elevation of everyday living in which man aspires to establish a relationship with God in life. As Abraham Joshua Heschel writes, "In Judaism, we experience the taste of eternity as eternal life within time."[37] From what we know, humans have only a limited amount of time to live life; given that crucial, scientifically observable constraint, we can still enjoy an existence in which past, present, and future are "real" and perhaps even endless, or as Heschel describes it, "eternal."

36. Durham, "*Shalom* and the Presence of God," 272–93.
37. Heschel, *The Sabbath*, 74.

Similarly, Martin Buber tells us that "the main purpose of life is to raise everything that is profane to the level of the holy,"[38] the "holy" being to improve the lot of humanity in everyday life. The prophet Micah refers to this in his question, "What does the Lord require of you?" The response is, "Do justice, love kindness, and walk humbly with your God,"[39] in which the Hebrew word translated as "justice" is *mishpat,* which signifies much more than "justice." It connotes an active effort, such as aiding the helpless and poor, to make things right, as well as to judge what is right. This includes all that conforms to the nature and will of God. In other words, *mishpat* is performing what is due—to act like God. This is the ultimate identification of one's self-conscience with the supreme selfness—with God.

As to the Hebrew word from which "kindness" was translated, the original, *hesed,* again means much more than its English replacement. It includes benevolence and compassion, of course, but it also entails an attitude of unfailing love and mercy in the spiritual sense. It is intended to reflect God's attitude toward humanity, according to the prophets. In Judaism, such biblical spirituality is not found in a monastery or in solitude, but rather in relating to the Hebrew Lord in everyday living.

Yet we live in an age where memories of the Holocaust are still alive, and deep human suffering abounds, while science has become our accepted source of truth. So could belief in a compassionate God concerned with humanity, the Hebrew "I AM" of the biblical prophets, YHWH, the God of Abraham, the God of Isaac, and the God of Jacob, make sense today?

38. Buber, *On Zion.*
39. Micah 6:8. JPS.

3

Spinoza: "God Is the Universe"

Under the guidance of religious philosophers, a noble god-conception is accepted by a large group. Then gradually the God worshipped becomes more personal and less cosmic until he degenerates into a mere celestial giver of gifts. Under the inspiration of certain spiritual idealists, prayers may begin in a particular religion as a mystic poetic communion, but it soon degenerates into a shameless selfish begging. The ethical life may be taught as a noble selfless idealism but it is quickly degraded into a cheap barter. All religions tend to deteriorate. The religion of Spinoza, too rarefied indeed for daily use, is the cold clear air which can ventilate every faith.

—GEORG CHRISTOPH LICHTENBERG[1]

BARUCH SPINOZA, THE FIRST person to take a philosophic and scientific approach in considering the Hebrew Bible, and Albert Einstein, whose biblical thought developed from that of Spinoza, provide us a bridge between the seemingly disparate, incompatible observations of great human suffering and a God concerned with humanity.

In 1656, Spinoza, the clever, twenty-four-year-old son of a prominent Dutch Jewish family, was also being excommunicated for heresy by the Jews of Amsterdam. Embittered, he never spoke well of Judaism thereafter, though he continued his criticisms. On the three-hundredth anniversary of Spinoza's excommunication, Israel's prime minister David Ben-Gurion

---

1. Lichtenberg was professor of physics, astronomy, and mathematics at the University of Goettingen in the eighteenth century. A sardonic but deep thinker, he is famous for his aphorisms, including this one, collected in many German volumes. Einstein cherished Lichtenberg's insights so much that in writing to Queen Elizabeth of Belgium, he offered to lend her his own book of them.

asked Amsterdam's Jewish community to lift it. They refused, and the excommunication stands.

Nonetheless, Spinoza pioneered biblical criticism from a philosophic and scientific standpoint, originating methods still in use today and expressed in *Tractatus Theologico-Politicus*.[2] He carefully framed disparagement of Christianity in seeming praise, though he was less circumspect about Judaism, which he overtly criticized.

Spinoza's father was a successful importer, and young Baruch Spinoza attended Jewish school to learn Hebrew and the Bible, which was taught from a Talmudic perspective, as is still done in Orthodox Jewish education. The Talmud, like the Christian New Testament, was written during a time of strong Greek cultural influence. On his own he studied secular subjects such as math, physics, and astronomy.

Brilliant, but with a rebellious nature, Spinoza questioned his teachers and their assertions about the Bible and its Talmudic interpretation. For example, Greeks believed in the soul as separate from the body, and this cultural belief made its way into Talmudic thought. But Spinoza argued that in the Bible, he found no evidence of either a "soul" distinct from the body or life after death. He said that angels do not exist but rather are merely visions, and that if God had a body, it would be the physical world.

Spinoza studied Jewish philosophers of the Middle Ages who tried to bring Jewish belief in accordance with secular knowledge of the time, but he refused to attend synagogue and—much worse—openly voiced his opinions, sealing his fate within the Jewish Dutch community.

From a Community of Marranos to One of Christian Dissidents

Amsterdam's Jewish community had recently been established by Portuguese refuges fleeing the Inquisition. The Roman Catholic Church in Spain and Portugal had been forcing Jews to convert to Christianity under threat of torture and death since the fourteenth century. Many Jews outwardly did so but practiced Jewish customs in secret. They were derogatorily called "Marranos," from the Spanish, meaning "pigs," in clear reference to the Jewish prohibition against eating pork. Spinoza was descended from

2. Editor's note: Originally published in Latin, anonymously, reportedly by Henricus Kunraht in Hamburg, though actually published in Amsterdam by Jan Rieuwertsz in 1670.

generations of Marranos. The Church in countries subjected to the Inquisition tried to ferret out Marranos so they could be "suitably" punished. After a few generations of forbidden practices and diminished observance, many Marranos no longer really knew Judaism, except for a few holdover customs preserved in the home.

Leaders of Amsterdam's Jewish community did not want to confuse these "new" Jews who were learning about their religion for the first time, nor did they want to jeopardize the Jews' position within pious Dutch Protestantism. So Jewish leaders offered Spinoza an annual stipend of 1,000 florins to shut up and keep his ideas to himself. Spinoza refused. He was thus banned from the community and ultimately excommunicated.

Spinoza was not alone in being ostracized from his community. Amsterdam's Christian community had far less tolerance for religious dissidents. The Church punished one of Spinoza's Christian friends and supporters, Adriaan Koerbagh, who publicly attacked Christianity. One judge urged confiscation of Koerbagh's fortune, amputating his right thumb, piercing his tongue with a red-hot iron, and imprisoning him for thirty years. Understandably, the thirty-five-year-old Koerbagh offered to recant, but he was sentenced anyway.

Koerbagh's actual punishment was a fine of 4,000 guilders plus 2,000 for the cost of imprisonment, ten years in prison at hard labor, then ten more years of banishment. (A typical professional annual income was about 600 guilders, so the fine was about ten times his salary.) He was sent to a harsh prison usually reserved for violent offenders and died within a year.[3]

While leading a mostly quiet life, Spinoza was determined to develop his ideas. He began discussing them in letters and lectures to small Christian groups. He could write pungently at times, and if his public speaking talent equaled his fervent writing, we can perhaps understand his appeal. For example, in his discussion of anthropomorphizing God, he wrote, "Theology has usually, and with good reason, represented God as a perfect man. . . . But in philosophy . . . we clearly understand that to ascribe to God those attributes which make a man perfect would be as wrong as to ascribe to a man the attributes that make perfect an elephant or an ass."[4]

A two-part book, likely published in Spinoza's lifetime and apparently assembled from his talks to his dissident Christian disciples, has this on its title page in elegant script: *Short Treatise on God, Man and His Wellbeing:*

3. Nadler, *Spinoza: A Life*, 268.

4. Spinoza, *Spinoza: The Letters*, Letter 23, March 13, 1965, 166.

(I) God and What Pertains to Him; (II) The Perfecting of Man So That He May Be in a Position to Become United with God,[5] indicating the emergence of these supporters. The text is as follows:

> Previously written in the Latin tongue by B.D.S. for the use of his disciples who wanted to devote themselves to the study of Ethics and true Philosophy. And now translated into the Dutch language for the use of the Lovers of Truth and Virtue: so that they who spout so much about it, and put their dirt and filth into the hands of simpletons as though it were ambergris, may just have their mouths stopped, and cease to profane what they do not understand: GOD, THEMSELVES, AND HOW TO HELP PEOPLE TO HAVE REGARD FOR EACH OTHER'S WELLBEING, and how to heal those whose mind is sick, in a spirit of tenderness and tolerance, after the example of the Lord Christ, our best teacher.[6]

The tone of the statement suggests that Spinoza's disciples did not necessarily achieve the psychological state of equanimity and humility generally associated with his philosophy, though the statement does attest to their devotion.

A Book Divulging neither Author nor Publisher

Spinoza continued his biblical critiques with a full book, though unsurprisingly he did not have his name—or any other—listed as author. *Tractatus Theologico-Politicus* thus appeared in 1670 as the first truly scientific criticism of the Bible. Spinoza tried to deceive anyone seeking to trace its origin by misnaming the city of publication as Hamburg (though it was more likely Amsterdam), but the name of the author soon leaked.

Written in Latin, the book was read internationally and created a furor. It was denounced by some, praised by others—and widely banned. Spinoza became so notorious that when an edition in Dutch was proposed, he himself stopped it in an act of self-preservation. How ironic (and sad), then, that Spinoza's stated purpose in writing the book was to promote religious freedom. As his preface reveals, such freedom was tenuous, if it existed at all at the time and in his part of the world: "If anything of what

---

5. Editor's note: Date of original publication is unknown; commonly used English translation by Abraham Wolf, published in London by A. & C. Black in 1910.

6. Spinoza, *Short Treatise on God*.

I say is deemed by them [the government] to contravene the laws of our country or to be injurious to the common good, I am ready to withdraw it. I realize that I am human and may have erred."[7]

Nonetheless, he set the theme and criticized bigoted Christian religious leaders in words still applicable today:

> Piety and religion—O everlasting God—take the form of ridiculous mysteries, and men who utterly despise reason, who reject and turn away from the intellect as naturally corrupt—these are the men (and this is of all things the most iniquitous) who are believed to possess the divine light! Surely, if they possessed but a spark of the divine light, they would not indulge in such arrogant ravings, but would study to worship God more wisely and to surpass their fellows in love, as they now do in hate.[8]

Using standards founded on Greek thought, Christian theologian contemporaries of Spinoza naturally judged the Hebrew Bible as wanting, ironically dismissing Hebrew teachings as part of that foundation. The result today is an insensitive interpretation of an already faulty biblical translation mired in Greek culture. Spinoza's criticism of these Christians is unbridled:

> Furthermore, if they did indeed possess some divine light, this would surely be manifested in their teaching. I grant that they have expressed boundless wonder at Scripture's profound mysteries, yet I do not see that they have taught anything more than the speculations of Aristotelians or Platonists, and they have made Scripture conform to these so as to avoid appearing to be the followers of heathens. It was not enough for them to share in the delusions of the Greeks: they have sought to represent the prophets as sharing in these same delusions. This surely shows quite clearly that they do not even glimpse the divine nature of Scripture.[9]

Actually, his remarks about the Hebrew Bible conforming to "speculations of Aristotelians and Platonists" and "delusions of the Greeks" represent a double criticism: one of Christianity and one of postbiblical Talmudic Judaism, both of which developed under a pervasive Greek cultural influence.

---

7. Spinoza, *Tractatus Theologico-Politicus*, 57.

8. Spinoza, *Tractatus Theologico-Politicus*, 53.

9. Spinoza, *Tractatus Theologico-Politicus*, 53.

As mentioned earlier, the Pharisees religious party was more influenced by Greek thinking than were the Sadducees in the few centuries after the Bible. In reaction to the Pharisaic adoption of belief in a separate soul and in life after death, the Sadducees underscored the fact that nowhere in the Bible was there a mention of life after death. Regardless, the Pharisees flourished and the Sadducees disappeared after the destruction of the second temple in Jerusalem.

No Sadducean literature survived. Our knowledge of the Sadducees is only through the writings of Pharisees such as the Talmud—not exactly an unbiased source, considering its Greek influence. So we do not know if the Sadducees proposed, for example, a biblical replacement for the question of life after death, as Spinoza himself would later suggest.

In fact, Spinoza always used "Pharisees" to specify Jews living in the centuries of religious turbulence that preceded both Christianity and rabbinic Judaism. He may have done so to distinguish their Greek-influenced beliefs from the purer Jewish thought of biblical times, or because of the standard, disparaging connotation that the word "Pharisee" carries in the New Testament and Christian community.

The Seal, "Beware"

Spinoza's connection to Christianity was not only through his references to the Pharisees but in his stated admiration for Jesus, though he rarely called him that; instead, he usually said "Christ." He wrote, for example, that "Christ" had received inspiration directly from God, but that Moses had only received God's word indirectly—through verbal transmission. He concluded, then, that "Christ's" inspiration was "higher." But this is a curious distinction, and there must have been a reason Spinoza preferred to use "Christ" instead of "Jesus."

"Christ" is a Latin word derived from the Greek, "anointed," which itself is a concept taken from the Hebrew Bible. When Spinoza wrote of "Christ's" direct divine inspiration, he also indicated that everyone could be so inspired. By saying "Christ," however, there is evidence that Spinoza was also being purposefully ambiguous in referring both to Jesus the man and to anyone in direct relationship with God. The question why he would do so, though, is again raised.

Spinoza was no dunce. He had no desire to again confront the established, government-sanctioned Christian community as he had the Jewish one and managed to be safely ambiguous. Additionally, he took other measures: in his often-denigrating religious commentaries written to friends, he affixed to his correspondence a seal with his initials "BDS" and the word *Caute* (Latin for "beware"), surrounded by a rose with thorns, as a cautionary reminder that they guard his letters near.[10] Letters could always fall into the wrong hands. His own reminder to beware was the signet ring he wore to make the *Caute* seal.

Ambiguity and inconsistency characterized Spinoza's life, in part due to his Marrano ancestry. Having to say one thing for survival while believing another had been his daily existence growing up and would not have been difficult for him.[11] Noted Spinoza scholar Yirimiyahu Yovel of Hebrew University said that he never forgot he was writing "largely for a Christian audience in an attempt to discredit their superstitions. . . . But to achieve his ends, he must ostensibly accept the principles of Christianity and argue from its point of view . . . a kind of Marranesque technique."[12] Indeed, Spinoza mastered it.

Discerning Spinoza's Beliefs from What He Said

What, then, did Spinoza really believe about the Bible? Spinoza felt that the Hebrew Bible was divine, in the sense that its writing was inspired by God acting through ancient Hebrews. Created, then, by human beings—along with their imperfections, prejudices, customs, and limitations—the Bible's meaning could only be determined by intensive study.

Spinoza also admired the Bible's ethical laws set forth by the prophets; he joined them in criticizing its detailed ceremonial rituals but did not accept the biblical doctrine that God is concerned with humanity. Rather, he said, "He who loves God cannot endeavor to bring it about that God should love him in return."[13] He conceded, though, that everyone can be directly inspired by God. Here he is restating the name of God given in Exodus 3:14; the "I AM" of God acts through the "I am" of the individual.[14]

---

10. A picture of Spinoza's seal on a letter to Leibniz is shown in Lessing, *Speculum Spinozum*, 283.

11. Yovel, *Spinoza and Other Heretics*.

12. Yovel, *Spinoza and Other Heretics*, 178. See also Strauss, *Persecution*.

13. Spinoza, *Ethics*, Part V, Prop. 19.

14. See chapter 1.

Jesus believed in the essence of the Hebrew Bible and sought to clarify its message, according to Spinoza, who nonetheless strongly rejected Christianity—the religion developed by followers of Jesus. Wisely, perhaps, given his penchant for enraging organized religion, Spinoza refused to speak about Christian doctrine publicly. He wrote instead in a private letter:

> I entertain an opinion on God and Nature far different from that which modern Christians are wont to uphold. . . . As to the additional teaching of certain Churches, that God took upon himself human nature, I have expressly indicated that I do not understand what they say. Indeed, to tell the truth, they seem to me to speak no less absurdly than one who might tell me that a circle has taken on the nature of a square.[15]

Spinoza developed an exceptional talent for raising topics of fundamental importance in his correspondence, prompting friends to exchange ideas that did indeed lead to his articulation of a unique understanding of God.

Spinoza's God—What He Is and Is Not

Spinoza is most admired today for *The Ethics*,[16] a book over which he labored devotedly for many years, though it was never published during his lifetime (despite mention in his letters that major portions of it existed five years before his *Tractatus*). It remains valued as a hard-to-understand masterpiece of thought—perhaps in part due to the great effort that must be invested to understand it.

In *The Ethics,* Spinoza's God has no anthropomorphic qualities but instead represents all "Being" in its ultimate unity. To humans, God has only two attributes: "thought" and "extension." In more familiar terms, we would call these "mind" and "matter." For Spinoza's God, all events—regardless of being past, present, or future—exist.

In another often-stated interpretation, Spinoza's God is the equivalent of "Nature" and thus leaves no room for the nonmaterial. But such a claim is based on a misunderstanding of his writing. Indeed, Spinoza himself unequivocally states: "As to the view of certain people that the *Tractatus Theologico-Politicus* rests on the identification of God with Nature (by the

---

15. Spinoza, *Spinoza: The Letters*, 332–3.

16. Spinoza, *Ethics.*

latter of which they understand a kind of mass or corporeal matter) they are quite mistaken."[17]

God, Spinoza explains, has an infinite number of attributes, of which only two (mind and matter) are within man's ken. God's other attributes are beyond our senses and imagination, beyond even what we understand as Nature. Spinoza's God, then, is much more than what we know—or can know—as Nature. God is a part of reality beyond human conception.

The Truly Wise Man Never Ceases to Be

While Spinoza does not support the thesis of a concerned God, he does assert in *The Ethics* that it is the nature of man to concern himself with God: "Every entity in the world strives to persevere in its being."[18] Among humans, this takes the form of an instinctive desire to preserve life, to somehow overcome death. Since past, present, and future coexist in the mind of God, death can be overcome by seeking to share the mind of God, by seeking the eternal in life. Spinoza called this attitude "the intellectual love of God."

Spinoza's "eternity"—or, to use his Latin term, *aeternitas*—is not achieved by living forever. Instead, it is achievable within a normal life span, as Spinoza explains in a letter to his physician friend, Lodewijk Meyer, by "the infinite enjoyment of existence."

Such enjoyment of existence is achievable to the extent that one's conscious thought is similar to God's eternal thought. This is possible, Spinoza says, because the mind is part of the body. Scientific research maintains that conscious human action, because it is determined by the mind, modifies the mind and therefore the body. When those actions are in accord with the ethical nature of God, the modified body shares in the mind of God and perceives the eternal.

According to Spinoza, there is no reason for such a person to fear death.[19] "The wise man," he writes in the concluding paragraph of *The Ethics*, "never ceases to be."[20] Rather he achieves eternity through his wise choices and wise actions.

---

17. Spinoza, *Spinoza: The Letters*, 332.
18. Spinoza, *Ethics*, Part III, Prop 6.
19. Spinoza, *Ethics*, Part V, Prop. 39, note.
20. Spinoza, *Ethics*, Prop. 42, note.

On Understanding Spinoza and Eternity

Unfortunately, these remarks on the wise man and eternity represent what is likely to be the most misinterpreted aspect of Spinoza's thesis. I say "unfortunately" because Spinoza considered the concluding pages of *The Ethics* to be the culmination of his system, so that to misunderstand those remarks is to misunderstand Spinoza.

In an attempt to clarify and put his thought in concrete terms, consider that the nature of human perception is essentially a person's awareness—accurate and real, or not—of the external world outside one's own own body. Einstein says that "the real is in no way immediately given to us. Given to us are merely the data of our consciousness."[21] We are thus left with the responsibility to perceive data in such ways as to reach the infinite enjoyment of existence: wisdom in our actions, allowing us to achieve eternity.

Georg Christoph Lichtenberg emphasizes the dichotomy between what we perceive and what we believe we perceive, once again regardless of "reality":

> To say we perceive *external* objects is contradictory; it is impossible for a man to go outside himself. When we believe we are seeing objects we are seeing only ourselves. We can really perceive nothing in the world except ourselves and the changes that take place in us. It is likewise impossible for us to *feel* for others, as it is customary to say we do; we feel only for ourselves. The proposition sounds a harsh one, but it is not when it is correctly understood. We love neither father, nor mother, nor wife, nor child; what we love are the pleasant sensations they produce in us. . . . Nothing else is at all possible, and he who denies this proposition cannot have understood it.[22]

Yet the love we feel in our minds for father, mother, wife, husband, or child is in accord with the mind of God—so the body modifications it causes are still part of God's *aeternitas*.

The human mind may have its physical basis within the confines of the body, but its range in thought extends well outside the body. When changes in the mind are brought about, which are also changes in the body, we may experience a level of awareness that becomes eternal, if the experience has

---

21. Einstein letter to Samuel in Samuel, *Essay in Physics*, 158.
22. Lichtenberg, *The Waste Books*, 123, Notebook H35.

been compatible with God's thought—or, in other words, if we have been, in Spinoza's terminology, "wise."

Extending awareness even further outside the body, yet still within the greater world of Being, is to become even more conscious of the self-awareness of others. This results in being able to empathize with them and thus come closer to the self-awareness of God. To Spinoza, this is experiencing eternity. As he puts it, "The mind is eternal insofar as it conceives things under the form of eternity."[23] Though seemingly circuitous, Spinoza's comment actually underlines the important function and role of the active, conscious mind in trying to attain the infinite enjoyment of existence—eternity not of the body but of existence.

The Ideas of Ancient Hebrews

Another view of eternity was that of theologian Abraham Joshua Heschel, who wrote, "*Eternal* is a moment of simultaneity of the human and divine, a moment in which God and Man meet."[24] Although articulated differently, this idea also reflects Spinoza's point that eternity involves such a unique relationship with God.

Characteristically, Spinoza derogated Jews in his writings but believed that his understanding of reality was consistent with Jewish tradition, as well as with that of Paul and ancient philosophers. He wrote (perhaps begrudgingly or as part of his regular inconsistencies) that "All things, I say, are in God and move in God, and this I affirm . . . together with all the ancient Hebrews, as far as may be conjectured from certain traditions, though these have suffered much corruption."[25]

Spinoza further declared that Jews had been chosen by God only in biblical times but were no longer the chosen people, and added, "I am inclined to believe that, with the opportunity afforded, since human affairs are notoriously changeable, they may again recover their kingdom, and God elect them to himself anew."

These words suggest that Spinoza believed the inner truth of the Hebrew Bible and the actions it ascribes to God, though he criticized its written manifestation. Spinoza stated that he believed it essential to know Hebrew in order to understand ancient biblical thinking: "And since all the

23. Spinoza, *Ethics*, Part V, Prop. 31, note.
24. Heschel, *Moral Grandeur and Spiritual Audacity*, 373.
25. Spinoza, *Spinoza: The Letters* (Letter 73), 332.

writers of both the Old and the New Testament were Hebrews, a study of the Hebrew language must undoubtedly be a prime requisite, not only for an understanding of the books of the Old Testament, which were written in that language, but also for the New Testament. For though the latter books were published in other languages, their idiom is Hebraic."[26]

Spinoza even started to write a Hebrew dictionary to facilitate his study, but he never completed it. He nevertheless sought to separate the Bible's true inner beliefs from temporarily expedient ones: "To avoid confusing teachings of eternal significance with those which are only of temporary significance or directed only to the benefit of a few, it is also important to know on what occasion, at what period, and for what nation or age all these teachings were written down."[27]

Spinoza further believed he had found "precepts which are eternal" to form the basis of his own philosophy. He wrote, "We clearly understand in what consists our salvation, blessedness, or liberty, namely, in the constant and eternal love for God, or in the love of God for men. And this love or blessedness is called in the Bible, 'glory'—not without reason."[28]

Spinoza thought that this "constant and eternal love for God" could be practiced by aspiring to live as if life were eternal, in the belief that it can be.

This unique understanding of eternity, *aeternitas*, may be expressed in the language of the Hebrew Bible as a sense of "holiness" in this world, a Judaic concept that continues to this day; it both defines and distinguishes ancient Hebrew beliefs from those of Christianity (and of most other religions).

Spinoza's writings thus resonated strongly with thinkers such as Einstein, just as many Jews today can connect with their ancestors of biblical times, thanks to the shared study and common understanding of unique precepts found only in the Hebrew Bible. Einstein clearly explained his personal connection, which is handled in more depth in the following chapter: "Spinoza's worldview is penetrated by the thought and way of feeling which is so characteristic of the living Jewish intelligence. I feel that I could not be so close to Spinoza were I not myself a Jew, and if I had not developed within a Jewish environment."[29]

26. Spinoza, *Tractatus Theologico-Politicus*, 143.

27. Spinoza, *Tractatus Theologico-Politicus*, 145.

28. Spinoza, *Ethics*, Part V, Prop. 36, note.

29. Einstein letter to Willy Aron, January 14, 1943, Einstein Archives, Princeton University Press, Princeton, NJ. Commentator: Encountered during Robert Goldman's research.

4

In Search of Einstein's God

Then there are the fanatical atheists whose intolerance is of the same kind as the intolerance of the religious fanatics.

—ALBERT EINSTEIN[1]

"THANK YOU FOR YOUR kind invitation. Despite being something like a Jewish saint, I have been absent from a synagogue so long that I am afraid God would not recognize me and if He did, it would be worse."[2] So wrote Albert Einstein in turning down an invitation from a Florida rabbi to attend services with his congregation.

Though he had scant regard for religious ritual, Einstein was fascinated by the word "God" and used it often in casual conversation. His close assistant for several years, Leopold Infeld, brought up in Catholic Poland, said he thought that Einstein used the word "God" more often than did a Catholic priest!

One of Einstein's more famous comments about God was, "I . . . am convinced He does not play dice,"[3] although most physical scientists today disagree with him. The late Stephen Hawking of Cambridge University retorted that "Not only does God definitely play dice, but . . . he sometimes confuses us by throwing them where they cannot be seen."[4] Whether Ein-

1. Jammer, *Einstein and Religion,* 97. Einstein letter to unidentified addressee, August 7, 1941, Einstein Archives 54-927. Princeton University Press, Princeton, NJ.

2. Einstein letter to Rabbi Isaac Hirsch, September 24, 1946, Einstein Archives 72-815. Princeton University Press, Princeton, NJ.

3. Calaprice, *Ultimate Quotable Einstein,* 380, Einstein letter to Max Born, December 4, 1926. Einstein Archives 8-180. Princeton University Press, Princeton, NJ. Editor's note: The complete quotation: "Quantum mechanics is certainly imposing. But an inner voice tells me that this is not yet the real thing. The theory yields much, but it hardly brings us closer to the Old One's secrets. I, in any case, am convinced that He does not play dice."

4. Stephen Hawking Quotes. BrainyQuote.com, BrainyMedia Inc, 2019. https://www.

stein or Hawking is closer to truth, though, remains unknown. Whether it makes sense to compare the two assertions is beyond the scope of this book, though it surely warrants future reflection.

Another of Einstein's statements about God is carved (in the original German) above a fireplace at Princeton University: "*Raffiniert ist der Herr Gott, aber boshaft ist er nicht.*" Usually translated as "God is subtle, but He is not malicious,"[5] I prefer a variation: "God is subtle, but He is not unkind." Einstein himself gave an even freer translation in 1946: "God is slick, but He ain't mean," the slang he used when told (falsely) that another scientist had disproved his general theory of relativity.[6] Notice that Einstein assumes God is on his side scientifically and would not trick him.

As it turned out, Einstein was scientifically accurate, but he did later concede to Vladimir Bargmann, "I have second thoughts. Maybe God *is* malicious,"[7] implying he thought God was indeed capable of tricking people into believing they understood things that, in fact, they did not.

In any case, not all scientists appreciated Einstein's frequent invoking of God. In fact, Nobel Prize–winning physicist Peter Kapitza was quite irritated by it and once snapped, "Einstein loved to refer to God when there was no more sensible argument."[8]

But what did Einstein really have in mind when he used the word "God"? Was it merely a picturesque manner of speaking in which he said "God" when he meant "Nature"? Or did he mean something more?

I believe that Einstein did not mean a personlike God. Einstein wrote of the human need for some transcendental explanation of reality, a need that most people seek in organized religion but that he himself sought in science. Yet in further discussions about whether or not he believed in God, Einstein stated that "there are the fanatical atheists whose intolerance is the same as that of the religious fanatics, and it springs from the same source. . . . They are creatures who . . . cannot hear the music of the spheres. . . . The Wonder of nature does not become smaller because one

---

brainyquote.com/quotes/stephen_hawking_131084, accessed May 13, 2019.

5. Remark made during Einstein's first visit to Princeton University (April 1921) as quoted in Clark, *Einstein,* ch. 14.

6. The ether drift experiments of D. C. Miller.

7. Sayen, *Einstein in America*; also found in Shapiro, *Yale Book of Quotations.*

8. Kapitza, *Experiment, Theory, Practice,* 350. Kapitza shared the Nobel Prize in physics in 1978.

cannot measure it by the standards of human morals and human aims."[9] In a letter to Joseph Lewis (April 18, 1953), he wrote, "I do not share the crusading spirit of the professional atheist. What separates me from most so-called atheists is a feeling of utter humility toward the unattainable secrets of the harmony of the cosmos."[10]

I believe that Einstein's God represented for him the wondrous, mysterious source of creation. The search for understanding the beauty of that creation seemed to afford Einstein a deep impetus for his scientific research.

What Einstein Believed

Einstein often declared that he believed in Spinoza's God. But as much as he revered Spinoza, he thought Spinoza's response to living in a suffering world was too abstract. Spinoza's solution had been to change one's view of life (by considering it from the standpoint of eternity), rather than to change life itself. Einstein felt that such an attitude may have been fine for Spinoza, but it would not work for ordinary people, as it amounted to a renunciation of life. And this was similar to a solution of pessimism—that is, Buddhism.[11]

But like Spinoza, Einstein also disdained contemporary organized religion, preferring a return to what he considered fundamental in life. Einstein supposed that any thoughtful person would reach his same understanding about existence, because he believed that deep reflection upon even diverse philosophical doctrines would yield the realization that they are more alike than different.

Einstein's personal library had many books on religion and philosophy—a substantial number on Judaism.[12] He praised Moses, Jesus, and the Buddha as mankind's greatest benefactors. With admirable impartiality, however, he considered *all* contemporary organized religions to be decadent—in fact, to have been in a state of decline since the days of the biblical

9. Jammer, *Einstein and Religion*, 97. Einstein letter to unidentified addressee, August 7, 1941, Einstein Archives 54-927. Princeton University Press, Princeton, NJ.

10. Einstein letter to Joseph Lewis, Einstein Archives 60-279. Princeton University Press, Princeton, NJ.

11. Einstein letter to Mr. Carl Colodne, February 27, 1938, Einstein Archives 33-295. Princeton University Press, Princeton, NJ.

12. I had the privilege of visiting Einstein's home some years after his death while his daughter Margot Einstein and his secretary Helen Dukas were living there, and its contents were still intact.

prophets Jesus and Gautama.[13] He held that the religions they inspired have fallen into the hands of entrenched, self-serving hierarchies more concerned with maintaining power than in pursuing Truth (though I would like to believe the organizational situation has somewhat improved since Einstein lived more than half a century ago.) He wrote, "If one purges the Judaism of the prophets and Christianity as Jesus taught it of all subsequent additions, especially those of the priests, one is left with a teaching that is capable of curing all the ills of humanity."[14]

This is consistent with his belief "in the mysterious God expressed in nature,"[15] as opposed to a personal or anthropomorphized God.[16] Einstein further believed in the power of Man to address our own social problems. As he explained, "If we want to improve the world, we cannot do it with scientific knowledge but with ideals. Confucius, Buddha, Jesus and Gandhi have done more for humanity than science has done. We must begin with the heart of man—with his conscience—and the values of conscience can only be manifested by selfless service to mankind."[17]

Einstein's Later Years

In the latter part of Einstein's life, his most creative physics work having been completed, he felt that the redemption he had sought in science still eluded him. He considered himself a failure because he had not succeeded in developing a unified theory underlying the forces of nature. We know today it would not have been possible to make real progress in doing so, because available scientific data at the time was insufficient. But Einstein did not know that, and he expressed his disappointment in a letter: "So it is imaginable that it is only chimera or fancy. Thus I am even worse off than our Moses because he could at least see before his departure that the promised land was before him while what I am seeing may be chimera. Well, so what—at least it is a beautiful one."[18]

---

13. In fairness to Buddhism, it did not begin as a religious faith. Gautama lived at a time and place when suffering was widespread, and it would have been very difficult to change society. He taught the reduction of suffering by meditation and turning inward.

14. Einstein, *The World as I See It*, 170.

15. Editor's note: Hermanns, *Einstein and the Poet*, 8.

16. Editor's note: Jammer, *Einstein and Religion*.

17. Editor's note: Hermanns, *Einstein and the Poet*, 92.

18. Einstein letter to Hans Musham, July 30, 1952, Einstein Archives 38-146.

He then turned more fully to the world outside science, his Jewish concern for humanity taking the lead. He told students at Caltech, "The concern for man and his destiny must always be the chief interest of all technical effort. Never forget it among your diagrams and equations."[19]

"Most scientists," he wrote to a correspondent, "treat conscience as a stepchild in their picture of the world. This is a kind of disease of the profession and one should always be conscious of this weakness."[20]

And on another occasion, he wrote, "Whoever shuts his eyes to avoid seeing the bitter injustices of our times, shares the guilt for their tragic continuation."[21] His words echo those of the Talmud two thousand years earlier: "He who can protest and does not, is an accomplice in the act."[22]

His focus on doing good for society came out in other correspondence as well. Einstein was highly concerned for social justice; he worked to bring more refugees—especially Jewish scholars—from Nazi-occupied countries into the United States. To meet immigration requirements, they were obliged to show guaranteed means of financial support when in America. Einstein vouched for so many of them using his own funds that the State Department soon stopped listening to him. The department claimed, rightly, that Einstein did not have enough money to provide guarantees for so many people.

Einstein's social activism extended beyond World War II and his support for Jews and creating the State of Israel. With his pacifist stance, Jewish heritage, German citizenship, and international fame, Einstein's firmly held social ethic gave him a unique perspective from which to publicly condemn racism.

From his friendship with W. E. B. Du Bois and support for Du Bois' newly formed NAACP to joining Eleanor Roosevelt's Committee for Justice and Paul Robeson's American Crusade to End Lynching, Einstein publicly decried what he called the "disease of racism." His activism earned him a large file at J. Edgar Hoover's FBI—a fact that came to light only many years after Einstein's death—and left him open to sharp condemnation and

Princeton University Press, Princeton, NJ.

19. Goldsmith, Mackay, and Woudhuysen, *Einstein*, 12.

20. Einstein letter to Yngvi Johannesen, September 13, 1943, Einstein Archives 55-409. Princeton University Press, Princeton, NJ.

21. Einstein comment on I. F. Stone's 1946 *Underground to Palestine*, October 27, 1946, Einstein Archives 72-799. Princeton University Press, Princeton, NJ.

22. Babylonian Talmud, *Sabbath* 54b.

mistrust from McCarthy-era politicians and leaders. Yet he stood his moral ground and challenged oppression to the end of his life.[23]

Hermann Broch: Flight from the "I" and "We" to the "It"

Einstein read widely, but in later life he wrote that he had given up novels due to lack of time. Yet he did read, and he was deeply moved by a novel written by his good friend, Hermann Broch, one of the many Jewish-born refugees Einstein had helped establish in the United States.

One of Broch's themes had been that science, in making our understanding of reality increasingly abstract, causes a breakdown in values, thereby inducing fear and anxiety. Influenced by Einstein's thought, Broch saw the theory of relativity as making possible an eventual reintegration of human values. In Broch's later years, he sought to develop a philosophical psychology that would provide humanity an "earthly absolute" to serve as comfort and guide. His "earthly absolute" included overcoming the fear of death by denying the reality of the flow of time.

The novel that Broch had begun in a German concentration camp and on which he continued to work while staying in Einstein's home for a time was his most ambitious book, generally acknowledged to be his masterpiece: *The Death of Virgil*.

The story takes place at a time of intellectual crisis not unlike Spinoza's or our own: people believed the old gods had failed. Virgil lived in the first century BCE,[24] when Roman paganism was crumbling. Broch writes of a dying Virgil who wants to destroy the still-incomplete manuscript of the *Aeneid*, on which he had been laboring for ten years.

With terrible clarity, Virgil sees in the last hours of his life that his work represented an effort to achieve only objective beauty, and that it would be used to glorify the oppressive political regime in which he lived. It did not reach for the truths of living that, by disclosing the divine in life, suffering man sought and needed. Broch wrote of Virgil's "supreme human compulsion" to "find a higher expression of earthly immediacy in

23. Jerome, *The Einstein File*.

24. BCE: Before the common era. Used since the seventeenth century in Europe, then by Jewish academics in the nineteenth century, I prefer it as a secular reference to the Gregorian calendar's "BC," referring to "Before Christ."

the beyond," and to "lift the earthly happening over and beyond its this-sidedness to a still higher symbol."[25]

In destroying his own work of "false art," because it did not point the way to that higher symbol, Virgil finally saw redemption for himself, but even more significantly, the removal of an obstacle toward redemption for humanity. Broch was saying that he believed that life's meaning lay in making a contribution to human society.

Einstein was uncomfortably stirred by the book, finding its theme apparently too relevant to his own life. He wrote to Broch, "I am fascinated by your Virgil—and am steadfastly resisting him. The book shows me clearly what I fled from when I sold myself body and soul to science—the flight from the 'I' and the 'We' to the 'It.'"[26]

Towards the end of his life, Einstein summarized what he had found to be the most important living truth: "Man can find meaning in life, short and perilous as it is, only through devoting himself to society."[27]

---

25. Editor's note: Broch, *The Death of Virgil*.

26. Einstein letter to Hermann Broch, 1945, Einstein Archives 34-49. Princeton University Press, Princeton, NJ.

27. Einstein, *Out of My Later Years*, 128.

5

Thinking About Time
with Einstein

What does a fish know of the water in which he swims all his life?[1]

—ALBERT EINSTEIN

EINSTEIN'S THEORIES OF RELATIVITY in 1905 and 1916 laid the groundwork for a new understanding of time that proved to have enormous implications in investigating the universe—and, as we shall see, in understanding the Hebrew Bible.

It is very hard to change the underlying tenets of our thought. They sit in the background of our minds, tyrannically determining how we think, though we are not even consciously aware that they are there. "To comprehend," wrote Einstein, "is essentially to draw conclusions from an already accepted logical system."[2]

Einstein wrote those words to introduce the ideas of another great original thinker, Galileo. To keep them in mind is of utmost importance in understanding what follows. Even when we take pride in believing that we are reasoning in the most logical and open-minded manner, we often are not. Each of us is limited by the subconscious assumptions in his mind—that is, by that "already accepted logical system" that defines our comprehension of a thing or a concept.

Our subconscious minds are full of assumptions about reality—our thinking is based on them; we build on them, and we could not even begin to think without them. Unfortunately, however, such assumptions are not always true.

For example, Einstein showed a century ago that our assumptions about the regularity of time—assumptions we accept without conscious

1. Einstein, *Out of My Later Years*, n.p.
2. Einstein wrote this in July 1952 in the foreword to Galileo Galilei, *Dialogue*, xix.

45

thought—are not accurate, as scientists have repeatedly confirmed through observation and experimentation in the physical world. Yet most people—educated and uneducated, professional philosopher and amateur, theologian and layman—blithely disregard Einstein's observations, merely to persist in reasoning on philosophical or religious matters based on a fundamental misunderstanding of time.

For those of us trying to comprehend the Bible, why is it important that we realize our instinctive assumptions about time are not true? *Because Einstein's new understanding of time—one that radically changes our knowledge of reality—is closer to that of the Bible than is our conventional understanding.*

A Common Error in Reasoning That Retards Scientific Progress

Einstein wrote,

Concepts which have proved useful for ordering things easily assume so great an authority over us that we forget their terrestrial origin and accept them as unalterable facts. They then become labeled as "conceptual necessities," "a priori situations," etc. The road of scientific progress is frequently blocked for long periods by such errors. It is therefore not just an idle game to exercise our ability to analyze familiar concepts, and to demonstrate the conditions under which their justification and usefulness depend.[3]

Traveling in Space and Time

Most of us see time as a smooth, riverlike flow from past to future in which we are immersed and in which only the present moment is real—the past no longer existing and the future not yet.

No, said Einstein. There is no uniform flow of time in the universe. The flow of time will differ for two bodies if their states of motion sufficiently differ.

The classic example is the story of twins, one of whom is an astronaut. If that twin were able to leave Earth in a rocket flying fast and long enough, she would return to earth noticeably younger than her twin. The astronaut

---

3. Born, *The Born-Einstein Letters*, 159.

may believe she has been away for two years and actually aged two years, but her brother who remained on Earth believes that ten years have elapsed and that he actually aged ten years.

Do not, by the way, expect to use this method of becoming younger than your contemporaries. Today's technology is not yet capable of building rockets fast enough to make the trip. For perspective, Russian cosmonaut Sergei Avdeyev was in orbit 748 days during three space flights. Physicist J. Richard Gott calculated that Avdeyev is now about one-fiftieth of a second younger than he would have been had he stayed home.[4]

The flow of time has another unusual quality, as Einstein realized, and as today's physicists understand it: the past, present, and future are all "real."

Among cosmologists, for example, the theory of time travel is not a matter only of science fiction but also one of serious scientific discussion.[5] J. Richard Gott III, professor of astrophysical sciences at Princeton University, writes: "In Isaac Newton's universe, time travel was inconceivable. But in Einstein's universe, it has become a real possibility. Time travel to the future is already known to be permitted [by the laws of physics], and physicists are investigating time travel to the past as well."[6] Gott reports that physicists who "build" theoretical time machines have succeeded in designing examples that permit travel into the future but only as far back into the past as the instant the time machine was created.

Will technologists and engineers in the far future have learned to build a practical time machine capable of permitting a person to travel into the future or into the past earlier than the time the machine was built? We do not know. In the design of a time machine that carries a person into the past, the traveler himself does not grow younger but continues to physically age in a normal manner. He would presumably be enclosed within a shell with a skin that separates him from the peregrinations of the machine.

---

4. Gott, *Time Travel in Einstein's Universe*, 75. Editor's note: Although correct when published in 2001, the days-in-space record has been exceeded by Cosmonaut Gennady Padalka: 879 days, ending in 2015. Commentator: After NASA astronaut Scott Kelly's one-year mission ended in 2016, his twin brother, former astronaut Mark Kelly, noted that "I used to be just 6 minutes older, now I am 6 minutes and 5 milliseconds older." Panel discussion at the ISS Research & Development 2016 conference.

5. Thorne, *Black Holes and Time Warps*, 483–523. Thorne, a pioneer in the field, is Feynman Professor of Theoretical Physics at the California Institute of Technology. See also Amtzenius and Maudlin, "Time Travel and Modern Physics."

6. Gott, *Time Travel in Einstein's Universe*, 5.

Russian-educated astrophysicist Igor D. Novikov, now a professor at Copenhagen University, explains that in prospective time machines,

> we ourselves cannot get younger in any "flight" voyage. In any one of us, in any human being and any system, time can only flow forward, only from youth to old age. . . . We know the law of increasing disorder, increasing entropy, which dictates the aging of an organism. (We could fantasize about a purely imaginative situation in which intrusive measures at the live cell level could prevent aging and even bring back youth, but this is a matter of controlling processes in living organisms, not of time flow.) The direction of the "psychological arrow of time" coincides, as we know, with this "thermodynamic arrow of time."[7]

But if such machines are built in the very distant future, eminent British physicist Stephen Hawking asked, not entirely facetiously, why aren't tourists from the future sightseeing among us? The answer: perhaps some are. Consider the news story of a mysterious stock market investor of unknown background who never loses and has become fabulously rich through speculation.

Consider also that this greedy investor from the future would not have changed history. At the moment in the future he decides to travel back, the story of his successful investing and its effect on the stock market would already be in historical records. This is an example of why the so-called "grandfather paradox" is no paradox at all.

A staple of discussion about time travel to the past, the "grandfather paradox" presents the case of a time traveler who goes to the past and murders his own grandfather so that he, himself, is never born. However, the past is fixed, not subject to change. If the murderous grandson goes back to some point in time, his visit there and what he does there would already be part of history when he embarks on the trip. No matter how hard he tries, the grandson with thoughts of murder cannot perform the foul deed, because it would not have historically occurred.

What is important for us in considering the Hebrew God and the Hebrew Bible is not whether practical time machines will ever be built but rather the relevance of assumptions by our era's leading theoretical physicists, including

---

7. Novikov, *The River of Time*, 235. Originally published in Russian. As of 1998, Novikov was professor of astrophysics at Copenhagen University and director of the Theoretical Astrophysics Centre, also in Copenhagen.

Stephen Hawking, Kip S. Thorne, and Igor Novikov.[8] These assumptions are: the past and future exist, and the past and the future are alive—as physically real as the present moment is to us right now.

The Lifetime Difficulty of Michele Besso

If you feel you cannot bring yourself to believe that the past and future both exist, you are not alone—in fact, you are in very good company.

When young Albert Einstein struggled with the concepts that would lead to his special theory of relativity and its new understanding of time, he discussed them while sipping drinks in cafes, smoking cigars in his rooms, and hiking across mountains with his good friend, Michele Besso. Besso tried to understand—he questioned and probed as Einstein explained his ideas. Einstein finally presented his theory in a deceptively unpretentious paper entitled "On the Electrodynamics of Moving Bodies."[9] Unlike most scientific papers, it was not studded with references—in fact, there were none at all. But in the paper, Einstein did acknowledge the help of only one person: Michele Besso.

Einstein and Besso also conducted a lifetime of personal correspondence, much of it about physics and philosophy. Yet towards the end of their lives, after half a century of such discussion, Einstein found it necessary to chide Besso for not truly accepting the reality of the past and future in his own understanding of the nature of the world![10]

In Einstein's theories, what we see as the three dimensions of space and one of time are not independent of each other. Rather, each dimension is an aspect of a unitary four-dimensional whole called "space-time." The separation between two events in space-time, usually called the "interval," can be divided into spatial and temporal components in innumerable ways. Though the interval between the events is fixed, its division between space and time components depends upon the point from which you view the two events. Einstein saw this four-dimensional characteristic of space-time in the special theory of relativity as rigid and absolute as Newton's space.

8. Hawking et al., *The Future of Spacetime*.

9. Editor's note: Originally in German, "Zur Elektrodynamik bewegter Körper," published in 1905.

10. Einstein letter to Besso, February 28, 1952, Einstein Archives 7-204. Princeton University Press, Princeton, NJ.

The time component, of course, includes past and future. Einstein wrote Besso to correct his friend: "It appears that you do not take the four-dimensionality of reality, but that instead you take the present to be the only reality. What you call 'world' is in physical terminology 'spacelike section' for which the relativity theory—already the special theory—denies objective reality."[11]

Generally speaking, most people, including scientists not working intimately with relativistic physics, similarly do not accept its tenets as part of their inner being either.

The Mysterious "Now"

"For myself there exists in the final analysis no becoming, but only being,"[12] Einstein declared. In other words, there is no "now" in the universe through which the future flows into the past.

By "being," Einstein meant four-dimensional being in space-time, within which three-dimensional change can, and does, take place. For example, Einstein said, "This naturally does not mean a negation of a gradual development of the organic world on the surface of the earth,"[13] because the organic world evolves as a gradually varying pattern in the fixed, four-dimensional picture.

We know that the universe is rapidly expanding. But if we look at it from a four-dimensional standpoint—length, width, depth, and time—it appears static, frozen. Nothing in this four-dimensional view flows or moves—it is what some call a "block universe,"[14] where time is charted by including not merely the present but also the past and future, so that all of it is in the model.

Therefore, an evolving object with movement, such as a star, would not be seen as a large or small dot, but rather as "star-lines, snaking along in the direction that corresponds to time, and also spiraling in a helix as the

11. Einstein letter to Besso, February 28, 1952, Einstein Archives 7-204. Princeton University Press, Princeton, NJ.

12. Einstein Archives. Princeton University Press, Princeton, NJ. Encountered during Robert Goldman's research.

13. Einstein Archives. Princeton University Press, Princeton, NJ. Encountered during Robert Goldman's research.

14. Editor's note: For further understanding of this theory, see Wharton, "Lessons from the Block Universe."

galaxy rotates."[15] In other words, it is not a snapshot of one point in time but rather a representation of *all* time.

Einstein was well aware that such a four-dimensional view of existence was hard to picture. In one of his many comments on the idea of God, he wrote, "The human mind is unable to conceive of the four dimensions, so how can it conceive of a God, before whom a thousand years and a thousand dimensions are as one?"[16]

But if time does not flow, why are we conscious of a changing "now"— a flowing present moment?

Yet there is no unique "now" in Einstein's universe. Consider, he suggested, two astronomical events A and B that are so widely separated in the universe that neither can affect the other. An astronomer on earth may observe event A happening before event B, while an astronomer in a distant planetary system may see B occurring before A. There is no single "now" flowing through the two events to define which is earlier and which is later.

More remarkable still, because the universe has no single "now," it is theoretically possible for an observer elsewhere in the universe, if he could discern such detail over such huge distances, to view all the events of your own life—past, present, and future.

In our everyday thinking, we find it hard to resist giving universal significance to the word "now." We may, for example, speculate on whether an intelligent civilization has ever arisen on a planet revolving about a star light-years away and wonder if intelligent beings are now alive on it. But "now" on that distant planet has so little correlation with "now" on Earth that the question is meaningless, in part because of the extreme number of years it takes for its light (and thus any other information) to even reach Earth.

To realize the poignancy possible in such a situation, consider a person on that faraway planet to be your father who journeyed there some years ago on a spaceship of advanced design through a shortcut in space, which cosmologists call a "wormhole," connecting two otherwise distant points in space-time. Is he now alive? Since you can only refer to your own "now," the answer can only be given in terms of your personal experience. No objective "now" coexists for you and your father.

"Now" is a subjective feeling, not an objective reality. We are touching on a mystery that Einstein considered to be impenetrable: the meaning of "I"-ness with its feelings of time-flow, and "now"-ness. There is neither

15. Wharton, "Lessons from the Block Universe."
16. Einstein, *Cosmic Religion*, 102.

flow of time nor "now" in the theory of relativity, as he believed them to be outside the physical picture of the world.

Philosopher Rudolf Carnap, who had discussed these matters with Einstein, reports that "the problem of the 'now' worried him [Einstein] seriously. He explained that the experience of the 'now' meant something special for Man, something essentially different from the past and the future, but that this important difference does not and cannot occur in physics. That this experience cannot be grasped by science seemed to him a matter of painful but inevitable resignation."[17]

It seems, therefore, that the concept of "I am" is as mysterious in the physical description of the universe today as it was thousands of years ago in the confrontation between God and Moses in the Bible.

Richard P. Feynman's Lecture on "Now" at Caltech

What we mean by "right now" is a mysterious thing which we cannot define and we cannot affect, but it can affect us later, or we could have affected it if we had done something far enough in the past. When we look at the star Alpha Centauri, we see it as it was four years ago; we might wonder what it is like "now." "Now" means at the same time from our special coordinate system. We can only see Alpha Centauri by the light that has come from our past, up to four years ago, but we do not know what it is doing "now"; it will take four years before what it is doing "now" can affect us.

Alpha Centauri "now" is an idea or concept of our mind. It is not something that is really definable physically at the moment, because we have to wait to observe it; we cannot even define it right "now." Furthermore, the "now" depends on the coordinate system. If, for example, Alpha Centauri were moving, an observer there would not agree with us because he would put his axes at an angle, and his "now" would be a *different* time. . . . There is no one who can tell us what is really happening right now, at any reasonable distance, because that is unobservable.[18]

---

17. Schilpp, *Philosophy of Rudolf Carnap*.

18. Feynman, *Six Not-So-Easy Pieces*, 101.

Questions for the Universe

Einstein's different way of thinking about time, compatible with what we know about the ancient Hebrew way of thinking about time, puts a different slant on questions about the world's origin and fate. Consider how modern physics would answer these questions: Did God create the universe? If not, how was it created? What was happening before then? Will all that humanity accomplishes be lost if the universe decays into a heat-death that can no longer support life? Does human free will have any meaning in a world of being in which past and future are fixed?

If we use today's understanding of the word "create," the universe wasn't created; it just *is*. Scientists who discuss the origin and evolution of the universe do so in terms of an initial event, though they do not explain how that beginning event came into being.

We cannot ask what happened before the world was created, because the words "create" and "before" refer to time, and time does not exist if there is no world.

Unfortunately, this is not a psychically satisfying answer. It does not satisfy our emotional need to seek knowledge of ultimate truths. So, can we use the word "creation" in an ultimate sense—one beyond time?

We can, but only if we drape its meaning in a mystery beyond our ken, because, with nothing with which to compare it, the concept is outside our ability to visualize. When we attempt to do so, we are taking our lead from the Hebrew Bible, which uses the special word for "create," *bara,* when it refers to God's creation of the world. But we cannot compare or further explore the conceptual meaning of *bara,* because it is never used in any other context in the Bible.

My earlier attempts to explore the concept of God in this work have been through the meaning of the name of God in the Book of Exodus: I AM. That name includes the ideas of consciousness beyond our own and a sense of selfness deeper than our own—both of which are matters of mystery to present-day science. It is thus humbling to realize that because the word "create" is beyond our ability to comprehend, the concept of God as creator deepens the mystery itself of God so as to become impenetrable.

Will whatever levels humanity manages to reach be lost when the universe can no longer support life? Those who ask this question tend to respond "yes," then add that this is a depressing thought.

Actually, it is rather optimistic, as it assumes that mankind will last that long without blowing itself up. But again, looking upon the world from a standpoint of "being"—in which past and future are real—rather than of "becoming," human history is not lost because nothing is lost: all continues to be. Even the word "continues" suggests movement in time, and in so doing it indicates our predicament: it is very difficult, indeed, to get away from our time-flow-based mental processes.

Is There Individual Responsibility in a "Block Universe?"

Can a person have free will in a world of being in which past and future are fixed? If not, can a person be held responsible for his actions? "Free will" has always been a tricky concept. Just what does it mean? In the nineteenth century, Friedrich Nietzsche considered free will to be a psychological fiction. As one would suspect, his view was sardonic:

> What is called "freedom of the will" is essentially the emotion of superiority over him who must obey: I am free, "he" must obey....
> "Freedom of will" is the expression for that complex condition of pleasure of the person who wills ... who as such also enjoys the triumph of resistances involved, but who thinks it was his will itself which overcame these resistances.[19]

Einstein also believed "free will" to be a meaningless term and tended to lose patience with those who used it:

> Honestly, I cannot understand what people mean when they talk about freedom of the human will. I have a feeling, for instance, that I will something or other; but what relation this has with freedom I cannot understand at all. I feel that I will to light my pipe and I do it; but how can I connect this up with the idea of freedom? What is behind the act of *willing* to light the pipe? Another act of willing? Schopenhauer once said *Der Mensch kann was er will; er kann aber nicht wollen was er will.*[20]

The translation of Schopenhauer is, "Man can do what he wills, but he cannot will what he wills." But Einstein believed that a person *is* responsible for his or her actions, and that this responsibility presents no conflict with the absence of free will. He replied as follows to a questioner concerned with

---

19. Nietzsche, *Beyond Good and Evil*, Section 19.

20. Planck, *Where Is Science Going?* 201. The quotation is from a stenographic transcript of a conversation with Max Planck and James Murphy.

the need to exercise human will in the effort to build a more just society: "I don't think that there exists a real conflict, because our spiritual tensions, not only those of the passions but also those of the urges to achieve a more just order of society, belong to the factors which, with all others, partake of causality. It doesn't represent an inconsistency if we connect those spiritual states with the idea of purpose and goal."[21]

To see why a future completely determined by past events (what Einstein called "causality") does not interfere with a person's feeling of freedom in making decisions, consider a disc on which is recorded a typical, action-packed motion picture.

When you view the story, you see the hero agonizing over decisions he must make in saving the beautiful girl from the dastardly villain. He makes those decisions rashly or intelligently, as he chooses. He exercises his will in what he believes to be a freely made decision. And it is freely made by all our ways of determination. But you, if you have seen the story before, know what he is going to choose, and that it is recorded later in the track on the rapidly rotating disc.

All the recorded episodes became real simultaneously during the manufacturing process, when the disc was stamped out by a replicating machine. Similarly, the past, present, and future are all real in the four-dimensional universe, which represents all objects' length, width, and depth simultaneously with all events of time. If only it were as easy to visualize space-time as it is to capture an entire story on a stamped disc.

You may choose to believe or not in freedom of will. But the possibility that the future is already here should have no effect on the choices you make.

We Each Play a Part in an Interrelated World

The Internet has both facilitated and made us more aware of the increasing interconnectedness of the world. Seemingly minor, remote events can have substantial effect on our lives through a chain of causes. The choices we make as individuals are, in fact, the result of innumerable causes, past and present, each of which plays a part and has been fed into and processed by

---

21. Einstein letter to Maurice Siguret, July 14, 1935, Einstein Archives 51-633. Princeton University Press, Princeton, NJ.

our brains. Our acts affect others, themselves becoming partial causes for yet others, some of which then affect us.

Each of us, then, is part of this great pattern of "interrelated being" on Earth. Because each part is dependent upon the parts to which it relates, each of us, if not repressed, plays more than a passive role in determining his or her own acts. Our acts thus help determine other parts of the pattern that in turn determine our position in the world.

Yet "external compulsion," said Einstein, "can, to a certain extent, reduce but never cancel the responsibility of the individual."[22] He saw physical reality as poetry we comprehend only in the most simplistic way: "We are like a child who judges a poem by the rhyme and knows nothing of the rhythmic pattern."[23]

Individual Striving Is Part of the Pattern of Being

Relativity maintains that time flows for the perceiving individual but differently for the rest of the universe. Your personal striving is part of the universal pattern of being—a pattern in which the surrounding world affects you but also in which you, if you are physically and politically free, can affect the surrounding world.

I believe that the idea of a deterministic space-time world can be more exhilarating than depressing; it offers room for individual creativity. It is also a world of all-moments-being, rather than of each-instant-fleeting. As such, it is a world in which the acts of daily living are not ephemeral but enduring, thus the opportunity to make one's own life meaningful is enhanced. Therefore, every individual act is a contribution to the structure of the world—which I find to be a sobering and humbling thought.

Einstein was aware that thinking in this deterministic manner was difficult and required high moral character. He wrote, "Spinoza was the first to apply with strict consistency the idea of an all-pervasive determinism to human thought, feeling, and action. In my opinion, his point of view has not gained general acceptance by all those striving for clarity and logical

22. Einstein letter to the Society for Social Responsibility in Science, July 19, 1950, University of Chicago, 27.

23. Planck, *Where Is Science Going?* 204.

rigor only because it requires not only consistency of thought but also un-usual integrity, magnanimity and—modesty."[24]

Do not assume, however, that we, with our ordinary souls of common purity and humility, are incapable of grasping these concepts. Realize that we will continue to struggle whether or not we succeed in understanding. If we do, then our greatness will be endorsed. If we do not, it will be because the concept itself is beyond our current human capacity. Recall that Ein-stein himself—the man who penetrated the physical meaning of time more deeply than any earlier scientist in human history—exclaimed in the last few months of his life, "Nobody knows what time is anyway!"[25]

24. Einstein letter to Dagobert Runes, September 8, 1932, Einstein Archives 33-286. Princeton University Press, Princeton, NJ.

25. Einstein Archives, Princeton University Press, Princeton, NJ., ca. 1955. This com-ment was part of Einstein's response in answer to a query about the amount of time required to create the world. Commentator: Encountered during Robert Goldman's research.

6

Death and the Hebrew Bible

In the way of righteousness is life,
And in its pathway there is no death.

—Proverbs 12:28

The Hebrew Bible does not speak of life after death. The Hebrews—as did Spinoza and Einstein much later—saw the universe, and their own lives within it, as a unity.

Only in the book of Daniel is there any mention of life after death—and that book was written later, during a period of strong Greek influence, and thus it had a different tenor than the other books of the Bible. Why were the ancient Hebrews not concerned with what happens after death? It certainly troubled the peoples among whom they dwelled.

Moreover, it is a natural anxiety of mortal beings. The oldest story known to humanity is the Epic of Gilgamesh, which is believed to date from the third millennium BCE. Its text was found inscribed on clay tablets excavated in Mesopotamia in the nineteenth century. In it, Gilgamesh searches for immortality but does not find it.

The Torah tells us that the Hebrews were slaves in Egypt, and we know that there was much contact between ancient Egypt and ancient Israel. The biblical scholar Abraham Shalom Yahuda showed that Egyptian cultural thought permeates the language used in the Pentateuch, the first five books of the Bible.[1]

Correspondingly, there are many Semitic words in Egyptian texts of biblical times.[2] In addition, one of King Solomon's wives was an Egyptian princess, and as the pyramids silently attest, the ancient Egyptians were

---

1. Yahuda, *Language of the Pentateuch*. Yahuda was a friend of Einstein who praised his scholarship.

2. Hoch, *Semitic Words in Egyptian Texts*.

obsessed with the problem of life after death. Yet the Bible shows no trace of such concerns rubbing off on the Hebrews.

Princeton biblical scholar R. B. Y. Scott writes that when the Wisdom literature in the Bible is compared to Egyptian Wisdom literature, much content is similar. He notes one striking difference: "the contrast between Hebrew ideas of reward and punishment in this life and the Egyptian view that judgment will take place in the hereafter."[3]

Writes the Ancient Hebrew:

Ill-gotten wealth is of no avail,
But righteousness saves from death.[4]
Says Wisdom: "He who finds me finds life
And obtains favor from YHWH."[5]

Writes the Ancient Egyptian:

Do justice for the sake of the Lord of justice . . .
Now justice lasts to eternity;
It goes down into the necropolis
With him who does it.[6]

Different Perspectives on Reward and Punishment

Some scholars claim that ancient Hebrews believed in life after death, with the accompanying rewards and punishment, but did not bother to mention it in the Torah because it was such a commonly accepted belief. Others claim the reason it is not mentioned is to differentiate Hebrews from the surrounding pagan peoples. These arguments not only make little sense in view of the critical importance of the known value that Hebrews placed on daily interactions and consequences, but they are also directly contradicted

3. Scott, *The Way of Wisdom*, 33.
4. Proverbs 10:2. JPS.
5. Proverbs 8:35.
6. Scott, *The Way of Wisdom*, 31–32.

in the Bible itself, which speaks of God's rewards as coming either in this life or in that of future generations.

In fact, the Bible tells us in gory detail that the ancient Hebrews—certainly the prophets and psalmists whose words we read—lived in no ivory towers and were well aware of life's vicissitudes. They fought both natural and political enemies, some even committing crimes punishable by death, and many witnessing the untimely deaths of loved ones. But the Hebrew Bible makes no mention of punishment after death nor of any afterlife.

Enigmatically, the Pentateuch in Exodus tells us that the names of noteworthy people are written in God's book, and conversely, those who sin against God are removed from it.[7] Again, though, no reference is made of consequences after death for the people themselves. So how are we to understand those words?

In the seventeenth century, the Catholic bishop of Meaux (France), Jacques Bossuet, offered his reason why the Hebrew Bible does not discuss life after death—an answer he clearly found satisfying. He declared it was because God did not consider biblical Jews intelligent enough to grasp the concept of immortality![8] We Jews have been accused of a great many things through the millennia, but lack of intelligence has to be one of the most far fetched. There must be a better reason.

That Mysterious Word, *Olam*

The key can be found in a mysterious word in the Bible that has no equivalent in the English language. Because there is not even an English phrase that precisely corresponds to it, *olam* is *always* mistranslated. That presents a significant difficulty, because the term occurs well over four hundred times in Hebrew throughout the Bible. The word is *olam*. Although its meaning is extensive (appropriately so), it is most likely derived from another Hebrew word that means "hidden."

If you look up *olam* in a good biblical Hebrew-to-English dictionary, you will find lengthy definitions—sometimes pages of them—for this single Hebrew word. One standard lexicon requires eleven pages of small print to explain *olam*.[9]

---

7. Exodus 32:32–33. Friedman, *Commentary on the Torah.*
8. Baclé, *Future Life*, 98.
9. Jenni and Westerman, *Theological Lexicon*, 852–62.

Even if we manage detailed explanations, the problem remains that nowadays, we currently divide reality differently from the way the ancient Hebrews wrote about their worldview over two thousand years ago.

Though we give the word *olam* many shades of meaning depending on its context, biblical Hebrews apparently gave it one that somehow encompassed many we apply today. If we can grasp that unique meaning to the level of being able to feel it, we will have gone far towards understanding the Hebrew Bible's lack of interest in what happens after death. In English versions of the Bible, *olam* may be found translated alternatively as "eternity," "world," "lifetime," "everlasting," "forever," "remote past," or "distant future." Yet neither individually nor collectively do any of these cover its full meaning.

The authoritative Hebrew-English lexicon based on the work of Gesenius[10] describes *olam* as concerning "long duration, antiquity, futurity."[11] Among its many meanings are the following: "of ancient time," "ancient people," "the long dead," "ancient hills," "forever," "always," "during the lifetime," "continuous existence," "everlasting covenant (with God)," "indefinite, unending future," "age (duration) of the world," "eternity," "everlastingness," "rock of ages," "from now and forever," and "as long as one lives."

Olam in Ancient Times and after the Bible

To add to the confusion in translation, *olam* underwent a shift in meaning after the Hebrew Bible was recorded. Biblical scholars Jacob Neusner and William Scott Green write that *olam* is "a concept that undergoes a distinct shift in meaning between the time of the Hebrew Bible and that of early Judaism. In the Hebrew Bible the idea of eternity is most commonly connected with God."[12]

Its meaning shifted from this deep theological one, discussed above, to being a secular term, merely denoting "forever." But for the ancient Israelite to live *olam* was to do the will of I AM, the Hebrew Lord.

This book is concerned with the original biblical meaning of *olam*.

For the ancient Israelite, according to Johannes Pedersen, a leading twentieth-century biblical scholar, "All events are connected because they contribute towards forming a psychic whole, into which they are

---

10. Brown, Driver, and Briggs, *Hebrew and English Lexicon.*

11. Brown, Driver, and Briggs, *Hebrew and English Lexicon,* 761–3.

12. Neusner and Green, *Dictionary of Judaism,* 208.

merged."[13] Furthermore, he says, the ancient Hebrews saw *olam* as a great whole into which all past, present, and future generations are fused and from which human events spring.[14]

Olam's most usual translation is "eternity," though not as an abstraction, such as the word "time," which abstractly denotes an indefinite progression through past, present, and future. Rather, *olam* is an "eternity" or perhaps a "continuity" and "interconnectedness" of living individuals sharing a united past, present, and future under God. To an Israelite "dwelling *olam*," as the psalmist sings, his sense of self, his "I am" therefore, is in a closely aware relationship with the all-encompassing "I AM."

Clearly, both because of the complexity of the concept and the lack of an existing cultural and linguistic context, any single English word or phrase that we might use to translate *olam*, especially in its ancient meaning, will be a distortion that does not capture its true sense. This often leads to English translations that blunt or even miss the point of the original Hebrew altogether. It would often be better not to translate the biblical *olam*, but to use the Hebrew itself. Consider these lines from the twenty-fourth psalm in the Jewish Publication Society's new version of the Hebrew Scriptures:[15]

> O gates, lift up your heads!
> Up high, you everlasting doors,
> So the King of Glory may come in!

It seems out of place to emphasize the durable carpentry of doors in a psalm of simple phrasing, otherwise focused on the relationship of man to God. How much more to the point the translated psalm could then be, if instead it were phrased as follows:

> O gates, lift up your heads!
> Up high, you doors to *olam*,
> So the King of Glory may come in!

The effect, I believe, is to focus our attention on the relationships, shared history, and ideal of the Hebrew *olam* as it exists in the past, present, and future of the Jewish people.

---

13. Pedersen, *Israel*, vol. 1-2, 475.
14. Pedersen, *Israel*, vol. 1-2, 491.
15. *Tanakh*, Psalm 24:7, 9. JPS.

Living in the Presence of God

The Bible, most strongly in the Book of Psalms, says that we can participate in *olam* to the extent that we do good and shun evil. We are then living in the presence of God—living in the world as "I am" while also aware of "I AM" within. In the imagery of Exodus, we are then being written in God's book, which, in the same context as the Hebrew *olam*, necessarily includes past and future. For example, in Psalm 41, the psalmist sings to God:

> You will support me because of my integrity,
>   and let me abide in Your presence forever [*olam*].[16]

The psalmist acknowledges God's support for his having led an honorable life in the physical world while also realizing that God has chosen him for an existence that transcends past, present, and future, which today we might interpret as part of Einstein's "space-time."[17]

Olam also appears in Psalm 37, where the first letter of each pair of verses in Hebrew spells the alphabet, serving as a memory aid. This suggests the psalm's importance to the people. Two of its verses read as follows:

> The Lord is concerned for the needs of the blameless;
>   their portion lasts forever [*olam*].[18]

> Shun evil and do good
>   and you shall abide forever [*olam*].[19]

Psalm 139:23–24 concludes with the psalmist pleading for redemption:

---

16. Psalm 41:13. Commentator: Here and throughout, *olam* is added in brackets in deference to Bob Goldman's preference for using the Hebrew word rather than its various translations.

17. Editor's note: Given our growing understanding of the relationship between time and space in special relativity since the time ideas in this manuscript were originally presented to family, friends, and Congregation Sof Ma'arav in Bob's early Torah comments, it appears that at least one similarity between Einstein's space-time and the ancient Hebrew *olam* has become clearer. The inseparability of "time" and "place" creates an all-encompassing concept, accepted in physics and understandable in the Bible. While the editor does not propose "space-time" as a translation for "*olam*," the notion of space-time is another tool with which to keep unraveling the ancient mystery of *olam*.

18. Psalm 37:18.

19. Psalm 37:27.

Examine me, O God, and know my mind;

probe me and know my thoughts:

See if I have vexatious ways,

and guide me in ways everlasting [*olam*].

Here, participating in *olam* carries the meaning of doing good and shunning evil. As such, *olam* was a term in familiar use as well as having an exalted usage.

For example, the First Book of Kings tells of Bathsheba coming to see her husband, King David, in his bedroom. He is close to death and is being nursed by a lovely young virgin. Bathsheba begs him to name their son, Solomon, as his successor. This act would be a great favor to her since David has sons by other wives and Solomon is not next in line of accession. David agrees, and Bathsheba exclaims, "May my lord, King David, live forever [*olam*]!"[20]

It seems, then, that the ancient Hebrews were not concerned with life after death because, as the psalms proclaim, they could achieve eternity, *olam*, in this life by doing what is right and good. They are then doing the will of God, living in the presence of God, and being written in God's book, which transcends distinction between past, present, and future. The language of biblical Hebrew sustains this understanding because it does not have tenses that separate past, present, and future. Instead, ancient Hebrew has two aspects that refer to events as either incomplete or complete, so both may refer to events in the past, present, or future.

This was a comforting belief for the ancient Jews. According to the Bible, the deeds that God favors—such as truly loving others, reducing the suffering of others, and treating others justly and mercifully—are in the realm of the eternal, along with the loving acts that others also have done for us.

As noted earlier, French Jewish philosopher Emmanuel Levinas believed that concern for others is more primary than concern for ourselves. He wrote that key in our human consciousness is anxiety about others' deaths, as this causes a deep sense of separation. Likewise, he said, "Time" is the deep relationship that humanity has with God.

The Bible provides a dramatic example of this notion in the story of Elijah and of Elisha who would become his successor, when they both knew that Elijah was about to be taken away by God. Elijah repeatedly told Elisha

---

20. 1 Kings 1:31.

to stay behind as he continued on, but Elisha was disconsolate about losing Elijah and responded with these words:

> "As the LORD [YHWH] lives and as you yourself live,"
> said Elisha, "I will not leave you."

> "As the LORD [YHWH] lives, and as you yourself live,
> I will not leave you."

> "As the LORD [YHWH] lives, and as you yourself live,
> I will not leave you."[21]

In repeating these words three times in nonsequential and separate verses, Elisha emphasizes that their relationship would not end with death.

The Meaning of *Olam*, Lost

When the ancient Jews, defeated in war, were exiled to Babylonia over two and a half millennia ago, (ca. 598–538 BCE), they found themselves in an alien land in which Aramaic was spoken. After their return to the land of Israel, they continued to speak Aramaic along with Hebrew. Though Hebrew, the language of the Bible, remained the more cultured language, it came to be used less and less in daily discourse.

Two centuries after their return, the Jews fell under Greek cultural influence that grew rapidly—Greece had become the dominant nation in the Mediterranean world. Aristocratic Jews began to find Hellenistic ways more stylish than Hebraic ones; these changes then spread to the common people. Greek ways pushed out older ones, so that speaking and acting Greek became the fashion. Hebrew as a spoken language continued its decline.[22] By about 150 BCE, for example, most Jews in Alexandria, then a leading world city with a large Jewish population, were unable to recite prayers in Hebrew.

By drifting away from their daily use of Hebrew, the ancient Hebrews' view of reality was also shifting, strongly influenced by subconscious factors arising from their changing environment, language, and experiences. For example, as Persians succeeded Babylonians within the relevant sphere of influence, the Jews gradually, possibly unaware, replaced their ancient

21. 2 Kings 2:2; 2:4; 2:6.

22. Barr, *Comparative Philology*, 38–43. Barr discusses the gradual decline of Hebrew as a spoken language and the loss in meaning of some biblical words as the Hebrew language itself changed.

biblical sense of time with that of the Persians and Greeks. Unlike ancient Hebrew, Persian and Greek (as well as other modern languages) have tenses separating past, present, and future, so that only the present moment conveys the sense of actual existence.

By contrast, verb usage in ancient Hebrew expressed a view of time compatible with Einsteinian physics—though only during the period in which biblical Hebrew was a spoken language—until about 300 BCE, when Greek became dominant. During that era, Greek culture was gradually erasing Hebrew culture (this occurred slowly from the sixth century BCE to the first century CE). Thereafter, verb forms differentiated time periods, just as they do today. The later Hebrew of Mishnah and Talmud actually used tenses the way we use them.[23]

As the Jewish understanding of time grew to be like that of the Greeks instead of their biblical forebears,[24] *olam* became an abstraction rather than an enriched fusion of past, present, and future events mediated by God.

Olam was thus no longer seen as a living reality. Eternity also was no longer seen as *olam*, attainable within daily life. Instead, the Hebrews saw eternity as merely an endless period of time.

It was during this era that the Book of Daniel was written—the only book in the Hebrew Bible actually discussing life after death, a subject that set off furious debate and spawned many Jewish religious factions. The Pharisees, for example, claimed that there was life after death. The Sadducees denied it, arguing it was not in the Bible. Foreign ideas of resurrection of the dead and immortality of the soul had entered Jewish thought from Persian and Greek sources—and to quite varying degrees, their influences remain today.

In this time of ferment, Jesus was born. Likely educated as a Pharisee, he preached biblical values to a people whose worldview was no longer strictly biblical. He did not teach "that the Kingdom of heaven was at hand (like John the Baptist) but [rather] that it was already a present fact.... The gospel he proclaimed was not a promise of future reward for certain beliefs about himself, but [rather] . . . a message of present salvation."[25]

---

23. For a discussion on the unique biblical understanding of time, see DeVries, *Yesterday, Today and Tomorrow*, 139, quoting Brockelmann, *Hebraische Syntax*, 37.

24. The Jews in this period spoke Aramaic as the language of the marketplace. Aramaic did not originally have tenses but eventually adopted them under foreign cultural influence.

25. Pringle-Pattison, *The Idea of Immortality*, 142.

Christianity did not adopt Jesus' beliefs on this topic and instead accepted those of the Greek-inspired Paul. Einstein, however, is purported to have said, "I have always believed that Jesus meant by the 'Kingdom of God' the small group scattered all through time, of intellectually and ethically valuable people." Einstein was likely referring to people throughout the ages who, like Jesus himself, had been taught that a meaningful existence was defined by doing good within our own lifetimes, and that we would be rewarded or punished depending on whether or not those good acts endured. Christianity's message, however, became one that delayed the reward to an afterlife.

An Inheritance from the Ancient Biblical *Olam*

The biblical emphasis on this life rather than on a next life—the belief that God is to be sought in the here and now, by the way life is lived—has remained a running theme in Jewish tradition, inherited from the ancient Hebrew *olam*. I believe this can be seen in the following examples.

Two thousand years ago, Rabbi ben Azzai said, "The reward of a good deed is a good deed and the reward of transgression is another transgression."[26]

A thousand years ago, Judah Halevi contrasted Judaism with the Islam and Christianity of his time, writing, "We do not find in the Bible: 'If you keep this law, I will bring you after death into beautiful gardens and great pleasures.' On the contrary it is said: 'You shall be my chosen people, and I will be a God unto you who will guide you.'"[27]

Nearly five hundred years ago, Baruch Spinoza strove to understand the original meaning of the Bible, consciously or unconsciously basing his concept of *aeternitas*, eternity, on the biblical *olam*. In the concluding proposition of his masterwork, *The Ethics*, his words succinctly summarize the nature of biblical salvation: "Blessedness is not the reward of virtue, but virtue itself."[28]

In our time, during Yom Kippur, the Day of Atonement, Jews attend synagogue and ask God to inscribe them in the book of life. This is not a request to live one more year, nor was it in ancient times. Jews, then and

26. Avot, *Ethics of the Fathers*, 58.

27. Halevi, *The Kuzari*, 75.

28. Spinoza, *Ethics*, Part 5, Prop. 42.

now, are calling on the Hebrew Lord to note that they are promising to live *olam*—lovingly, justly, and mercifully—that is, live in a way that allows them to participate in the eternal.

Olam Rediscovered

A century ago, Einstein initiated a remarkable change in the scientific understanding of time that has yet to have a radical impact on the way most people think. Past and future are real in the universe; there is no objective "now."[29] Thus, it is not just the present moment that has reality. Although past, present, and future remain separate within an individual's consciousness, in a higher unity they coexist. Unexpectedly, the ancient Hebrew view of time conforms to Einstein's revolutionary understanding of physical reality more closely than does our conventional view.

When Einstein's friend Michele Besso died shortly before he did, Einstein sent his dear friend's family a note that included these words: "And now he has preceded me briefly in bidding farewell to this strange world. This signifies nothing. For us believing physicists, the distinction between past, present, and future is only an illusion, even if a stubborn one."[30]

The ancient biblical understanding of *olam* predates a spiritual tumult and confusion that radically changed its meaning over two millennia ago. With Albert Einstein's contributions in the twentieth century, *olam* has gained scientific respectability. It can now underlie the basic thought processes of modern man and woman as they consider the eternal, using a biblical way of thinking in intellectually acceptable ways.

29. See Georbran, "Einstein and the Fabric of Time."
30. Quoted in Hoffman, *Albert Einstein*, 257–8.

A Medical Scientist Reflects on the Death of His Father

After he died, it was impossible for me to imagine my father as disintegrated into nothingness ... that that body was now matter, inanimate matter, dispersed in the soil as atoms of carbon and nitrogen, hydrogen and sulfur. And nothing more.

His presence was felt by me every day, sometimes at unexpected moments, triggered by an event that stirred my memory, but more often deliberately invoked. I conjured his presence and created a dialogue in my mind, providing answers to my questions framed in his words and voice. As time passed and the particulars of my life became more removed from those I had shared with him, I strained to articulate what he would say, how he would say it, why he would say it. I knew it to be a fantasy, a form of psychological comfort for a loss that would never be overcome, that should never be overcome, for who willingly lets go of such deep and unconditional love?

But then I began to wonder whether there was a dimension where he actually still existed, and whether his thoughts and feelings I had conjured up, were only a delusion, a psychological balm, a convenient mechanism to draw upon the wisdom and insight he had shared with me. Could these ideas and senses possibly come from another place, the place where human science and rationality find their limits, the place where speculation ends?[31]

---

31. Groopman, *Measure of Our Days*, 25–26. Dr. Jerome Groopman is professor of immunology at Harvard Medical School and chief of Experimental Medicine at Beth Israel Deaconness Medical Center.

7

A Jew, a Christian, a Hindu
. . . and God

Belief is desecrated when given to unproved and unquestioned
statements for the solace and private pleasure of the believer.

—WILLIAM KINGDON CLIFFORD[1]

JEWISH PHILOSOPHER SAMUEL ALEXANDER delivered two remarkable sets
of lectures entitled "Space, Time and Deity"[2] at the University of Glasgow,
1917–1918. They were presented as part of the Gifford Lectures, established
in 1885 to support noteworthy scholars who spoke to other academicians
as well as to the public for the stated purpose of "Promoting, Advancing,
Teaching, and Diffusing the study of Natural Theology, in the widest sense
of that term, in other words, The Knowledge of God."[3]

Lord Gifford stipulated that lecturers must "treat their subject as
a strictly natural science, the greatest of all possible sciences, indeed, in
one sense, the only science, that of Infinite Being, without reference to or
reliance upon any supposed special exceptional or so-called miraculous
revelation."[4]

Alexander was the first Jew to obtain a fellowship at any Oxford college
and went on to a professorship at the University of Manchester in 1893.[5]

1. Quoted by William James in his essay, "The Will to Believe," section 2. The essay
was first published in June 1896. James describes Clifford, a young English philosopher,
as a "delicious *enfant terrible.*" Evidently he was very well known in James' day; James
refers to him often and by his last name only.

2. Alexander, *Space, Time, and Deity.*

3. Editor's note: Although Lord Adam Gifford bequeathed funds to Edinburgh,
Glasgow, Aberdeen, and St. Andrews in his will in 1885, the Gifford Lectures did not
begin until 1888.

4. From Lord Gifford's will.

5. England had religious restrictions on higher education until legislation enacted

He was beloved and respected there for decades, and, along with other pioneering professors, actively worked to make it an exciting center for scientific research. In physics, for example, Ernest Rutherford discovered the atomic nucleus, creating the science of nuclear physics. In behavioral psychology, C. Lloyd Morgan was developing ideas that would lead to his full theory of emergent evolution.[6]

Alexander was deeply influenced by Morgan's ideas of emergence in evolutionary development, and the two men became lifelong friends. Alexander's Gifford Lecture was the culmination of their discussions, from which he developed his science-based philosophy.[7] In *Space, Time and Deity*, Alexander described the evolution of the universe through the concept of space-time. He explained his idea of "steps" of evolution, from which progressively higher levels of existence develop, until, after innumerable steps, humanity emerges. Then evolution continues beyond the level of humanity to the next step, which he calls "Deity."

Alexander also spoke in 1931, at a series of lectures sponsored by the British Broadcasting System. Other speakers included England's leading thinkers, whose work concerned the relation between science and religion. Among the distinguished participants were Julian Huxley, J. S. Haldane, Bronislaw Malinowski, and Arthur Eddington. On this occasion, Alexander again presented his beliefs on Nature and God:

> Nature is historical and grows so as to present in time a series of emergent qualities of which mind is the highest that we know from direct experience of ourselves or other selves. Why should this process stop? The mere outgrowth of life from matter, and matter from life, each quality resting upon a body characterized by the distinctive quality of the lower level of existence, suggests a further quality of existence beyond mind, which is related to mind as mind to life or life to matter. That quality I call deity, and the being which possesses it is God.
>
> . . . If you ask me what God is, I can only answer he is a being whose body is the whole world of nature. . . . The God who is the object of religious feeling is not a fancy embodied under

---

in 1870. Alexander received his Oxford fellowship in 1882. As to be expected for the time, he encountered substantial anti-Semitism at Oxford.

6. Morgan, *Emergent Evolution*.

7. Morgan presented his ideas during the 1922 Gifford lectures, which he began by describing Alexander's thoughts.

some mood of excitement, but has its basis in solid fact and in the general nature of things.[8]

Descartes on Man's Possible Growth Towards God

In the seventeenth century, René Descartes, famed for the observation, "I think, therefore I am,"[9] also meditated on his potential to evolve beyond his humanity into a being like God, foreshadowing both Samuel Alexander's lectures and Charles Darwin's *The Origin of Species*[10] by more than 250 years.

Descartes wrote in 1641,

[P]erhaps I am something more than I suppose myself to be, and it may be that all those perfections which I attribute to God, in some way exist potentially in me, although they do not yet show themselves, and are not reduced to act.

Indeed I am already conscious that my knowledge is being increased [and perfected] by degrees; and I see nothing to prevent it from thus gradually increasing to infinity, nor any reason why, after such increase and perfection, I should not be able thereby to acquire all the other perfections of the Divine nature. . . .

Yet on looking more closely into the matter, I discover that this cannot be; for, in the first place, although it were true that my knowledge daily acquired new degrees of perfection, and although there were potentially in my nature much that was not as yet actually in it, still all these excellencies make not the slightest approach to the idea I have of the Deity.[11]

Creative Evolution

In developing his system, Alexander read French philosopher Henri Bergson, whose 1914 Gifford lectures (four years before Alexander) maintained that evolution was directed by an immaterial élan vital. This was a creative

---

8. *Science and Religion*, 136.

9. From Descartes' *Discourse on Method*.

10. Darwin, *Origin of Species*.

11. Descartes, *Meditation III*.

impulse, which embraced evolution's full range, from its beginning to the establishment of human consciousness, but no further. Bergson described his ideas in *Creative Evolution,* which included a concept of time reminiscent of Einstein's theory of special relativity, published in 1905. Bergson's book appeared two years later in France, then was published in English in 1911. He wrote, "In reality the past is preserved by itself automatically. In its entirety, probably, it follows us at every instant, all that we have felt, thought, and willed from our earliest infancy is there, leaning over the present which is about to join it, pressing against the portals of consciousness that would fain leave it outside."[12]

Bergson's ideas veered towards Catholicism, though he was born of Jewish parents, and in 1914 he became the first Jewish member of the Académie française. But his writings, especially *Creative Evolution,* were denounced and banned by the Catholic Church. Towards the end of his life, living in German-conquered France, Bergson refused an exemption from the prevalent anti-Semitic laws. Instead, in 1940, he declared himself to be a Jew.

A Catholic and a Hindu with Similar Ideas

The Christian: Teilhard de Chardin

After the First World War in France, Jesuit paleontologist Pierre Teilhard de Chardin articulated a view that scientific evolution in the universe proceeded towards what he called the "Omega Point," a concept named after the last letter of the Greek alphabet. He believed that God had a hand within this Omega, drawing towards Him the entire evolutionary process, and that the final goal of evolution was divinity as exemplified in "a universal Christ." He said he was influenced by Bergson's *Creative Evolution,* and he was also likely familiar with Alexander's writings.

Yet Teilhard de Chardin's early work, such as *Cosmic Life,*[13] was a pantheistic vision, as he began to merge his interest in mankind, the universe, and God. In 1929, while working as a paleontologist in China, he

12. Bergson, *Creative Evolution.*

13. Editor's note: Most of Teilhard de Chardin's other writings did not appear in print until after his death, since the Church forbad him to publish or lecture on religious matters beginning in 1926. *Cosmic Life* came out in 1959, several years after his death, though like his other works, manuscript copies were likely distributed among his friends and colleagues during his lifetime.

wrote *The Divine Milieu*, in which he described the divine as pervading the physical world. A decade later, in *The Phenomenon of Man*,[14] Teilhard described his evolutionary history of the universe and the human species as evolving towards consciousness and the Omega Point, concluding that the only universe capable of containing the human person is an irreversibly "personalizing" universe.[15]

Unfortunately, Teilhard would never learn how popular his work would become; the Catholic Church, finding his thoughts of evolution dangerous, had forbidden him, as a Jesuit, to publish them during his lifetime.

His ideas, often expressed through neologisms, which many found fanciful and difficult to understand, were defended by some scientists and attacked by others. Prominent English biologist Julian Huxley, for example, appreciated Teilhard's way of thinking, though he frequently acknowledged its complexity. In his introduction to the English edition of *The Phenomenon of Man*, Huxley qualified his explanations with phrases such as, "If I understand him aright," "Here his thought is not fully clear to me," and "Though many scientists may, as I do, find it impossible to follow him all the way."[16] Today this work continues to be admired by some, reviled by others, and difficult to understand by virtually everyone.

The Hindu: Sri Aurobindo

Around the same time, a brilliant Hindu religious thinker in India, Sri Aurobindo, wrote influential books on the search for and evolution of the self. Born in Calcutta but educated in England, he excelled in Greek and Latin and taught himself German and Italian.

In 1893, Aurobindo returned to India, where he was employed in the service of the maharajah, learning Sanskrit and absorbing Indian culture. He became professor of English and French, then vice-principal of Baroda College. In 1900, he fought for India's independence and spent a year in jail, partly in solitary confinement. There he practiced Yoga, meditated, and studied the *Bhagavad Gita* and the *Upanishad*[17]—texts he considered the

14. Teilhard, *The Phenomenon of Man*.

15. Teilhard, *The Phenomenon of Man*, 290.

16. Teilhard, *The Phenomenon of Man*, 18, 19.

17. Editor's note: The *Bhagavad Gita* is part of the *Mahabharata*, an ancient Sanskrit epic (800–400 BCE). It includes Krishna's teachings on the soul and how to approach life. The *Upanishads* are philosophical texts on Hinduism, spiritual, and inner teachings:

source of his major ideas on the self. In ancient Hindu writings, the self is sought within the all-encompassing eternal Self.

From 1914 to 1921, Aurobindo published a philosophical monthly, the *Arya,* in which most of his important works appeared serially. He believed that the human mind could spiritually advance in time toward a uniting Supermind. He wrote,

> Evolution is the process by which it [the divinity within us] liberates itself; consciousness appears in what seems to be inconscient, and once having appeared is self-impelled to grow higher and higher and at the same time to enlarge and develop toward a greater and greater perfection. Life is the first step of this release of consciousness; mind is the second. But the evolution does not finish with mind; it awaits a release into something greater, a consciousness which is spiritual and supramental. The next step of the evolution must be toward the development of Supermind.[18]

Both Aurobindo in his "Supermind" (evolved self-awareness through Divine Knowledge) and Teilhard in his "Omega Point" (evolutionary divinity) determined that these higher states of mind already exist objectively; they do *not* evolve from human consciousness. In contrast, Alexander found that scientific theories of evolution of the universe supported his idea that humans are evolving towards a new level of being, towards deity.

In *Space, Time and Deity,* Alexander writes that "in its relation to conduct, religion does not so much command us to perform our duties with the consciousness that they are the commands of God, as rather it is religion to do our duty with the consciousness of helping to create his deity."[19] In Alexander's system, the evolved deity is not a caring God concerned with individual persons, as is the God of the Hebrew Bible.

The difference in these perspectives is profound. Yet all are based on a scientific understanding of evolution at the intellectual, spiritual, and/or physical levels. So in the chapters ahead, I argue that today's science is not only compatible with Alexander's idea of progress towards and creation of deity but that science also enables us to go further in reasonable conjecture: evolutionary progress, such as the kind Alexander describes, takes us towards

---

self-realization, Yoga, meditation, karma, reincarnation. The earliest *Upanishad* dates from about 500 BCE and serves as the basis for the Hindu religion.

18. Aurobindo, *The Mind of Light,* 21. This slim volume (106 pages) should not be confused with Aurobindo's major philosophical work, *The Mind of Light,* an 1,100-page exposition.

19. Alexander, *Space, Time and Deity.*

a God concerned with each person, provided that people behave in a certain manner—though humans have not yet mastered this behavior.

A Request to the Reader

Consider how mightily science has progressed in the century since Alexander wrote on the topic of deity. Einstein's theories were still novel back then, yet they are accepted as genius today. Evolutionary biology was but dimly understood a hundred years ago, and systems theory did not exist at all. Yet the essence of these concepts is that humans and our understanding can evolve—and arguably have done so—on many levels, notably towards the deity described in the Hebrew Bible.

Many readers may be tempted to stop here. To a rational nonfundamentalist, the prospect of a God concerned with the individual may appear scientifically outrageous. To a Christian or Jewish biblical literalist, evolutionary progress towards such a God may appear religiously shameful. I contend that, though conjectural, my statements are neither outrageous nor shameful.

I have seriously heeded Clifford's cautionary words in this chapter's epigraph, "Belief is desecrated when given to unproved and unquestioned statements for the solace and private pleasure of the believer." I now ask that the reader keep an open mind as I explain the case for evolutionary progress towards a God concerned with all persons.

8

Evolution, Empathy, Emergence

Perhaps, in time, the so-called Dark Ages will be thought of
as including our own.

—Georg Christoph Lichtenberg[1]

Evolution: From Inauspicious Beginnings to the Human Mind

WE ARE THE CHILDREN of evolution. More than three billion years ago, some inorganic material organized itself into a primitive entity that exhibited the properties of life. Among the properties that emerged were the ability to reproduce and the drive to evolve, in association with similar entities, into something more complex. That resulting entity also eventually combined with similar ones, which in turn generated something still more complex.

This process of self-organization with the emergence of new, richer properties repeated along many paths. Some of these came to an end when the evolved entity was unable to survive long enough to reproduce. Other entities continued in innumerable steps for thousands of millions of years of evolution until today. One of those paths resulted in the human brain.

It is flattering to think that the human brain is the most complex structure known to exist. It is made up of about a hundred billion cells, some of which are called neurons, interacting in an intricate tangle of communication paths. The connectors between neurons are called synapses; a single neuron has, on average, ten thousand synapses, and the brain as a whole has hundreds of trillions of these neural connections, at the potential rate of 100 trillion to 20 quadrillion per second.[2]

1. Lichtenberg lived in eighteenth-century Germany. Unfortunately, his words still apply.

2. Editor's note: Current statistics on neural activity are as close to the time of publication as possible. Stanford Neuroblog, "Ask a Neuroscientist."

Somehow, from this dense network that weighs only about three pounds, consciousness emerges. The human brain becomes the human mind, aware of itself and of other minds, able to control how some of its brain cells interact,[3] and able to communicate with either one or many other minds at once.

What Is Emergence?

Each advance in the evolution of the brain was caused by emergence of new qualities from an earlier stage of development. How does this happen? The daunting answer: nobody knows. No one understands why this drive in nature toward greater complexity through steps of convergence, self-organization, and emergence again occurs. But it is the way the universe works.

Emergence is the phenomenon of new, often completely different characteristics arising from a dynamic, complex organization of features acting in unity. It is considered so common in nature that a field researcher once observed, "It seems difficult for any densely-connected aggregate to escape emergent properties."[4] In fact, emergence is found in complex artificial systems as well as natural physical ones, and it is studied widely on an interdisciplinary basis as an aspect of the new field of complexity theory.[5] Scientists still do not know how or why there is a drive toward greater complexity through convergence, self-organization, and emergence. But it appears that the universe does indeed work this way.

Some people (especially professional cynics unfamiliar with recent scientific developments) have derided the very notion of emergence as "mysterious and mystical" and therefore unreal. But a Princeton-published textbook on biological systems states,

> Self-organization studies have shown that the implementation of simple behavioral rules by large numbers of components in a system can yield unexpected structures and events not present at the level of the individual components. Because the global (collective) properties of the system often deny intuitive understanding of their origins, those properties may seem to appear

3. Many experimental studies have identified areas of the brain controlled by specific types of thought and action. Editor's note: See Blood and Zatorre, "Intensely Pleasurable Responses to Music," 11818–23.

4. Valera et al., *The Embodied Mind*, 90.

5. See Waldrop, *Complexity: The Emerging Science*.

mysteriously. There is nothing mystical or unscientific about their appearance however.[6]

> ## The Tables Turned
>
> Sweet is the lore which nature brings;
> Our meddling intellect
> Mis-shapes the beauteous forms of things
> We murder to dissect.
>
> —WILLIAM WORDSWORTH[7]

A familiar example of emergence is in the case of water, which consists simply of two atoms of hydrogen and one of oxygen, but which nevertheless exhibits emergent properties. For example, the temperature at which water freezes or liquefies cannot be predicted based on the properties of its atomic makeup.

Emergent characteristics are also observable among social insects, such as in an ant colony. A single ant has very limited capability, but the colony as a whole has developed the ability to gather, grow, and store food, reproduce, enlarge the nest, repel enemies, and do what is necessary to thrive.

Robert B. Laughlin, who was awarded the Nobel Prize in physics in 1998, believes his field is at the threshold of a new era that will be even more promising than the present one, in which emergence has already played a major role. He writes, "I think that a good case can be made that science has now moved from an age of reductionism to one of emergence, a time when the search for the ultimate cause of things shifts from the behavior of parts to the behavior of the collective."[8]

Evolutionary biologists such as Harvard's Ernst Mayr were drawn to the study of emergence even before physicists. In 1982, Mayr wrote that living systems "almost always have the peculiarity that the characteristics of the whole cannot (not even in theory) be deduced from the most

---

6. Camazine et al., *Self-Organization in Biological Systems*, 31–32. The international group of authors includes scholars from the Université Libre de Bruxelles in Belgium, University of Bristol in England, Massey University in New Zealand, and Paul Sabatik University in France.

7. Seventh of eight stanzas in Wordsworth's poem, "The Tables Turned," 1798.

8. Laughlin, *A Different Universe*, 208.

complete knowledge of components, taken separately, or in other partial combinations. This appearance of new characteristics in wholes has been designated emergence."[9]

Then in 2004, backed by twenty years of additional progress in experimental biology, Mayr wrote further:

> For working scientists, emergence of something qualitatively new is a daily encountered fact of life. They have no difficulty with this phenomenon because they know that the properties of higher systems are due not exclusively to the properties of the components but also to the ordering of these systems. . . .
>
> It is now abundantly clear that evolutionary emergence is an empirical phenomenon without any metaphysical foundations. Acceptance of this principle is important because it helps explain phenomena that previously had seemed to be in conflict with a mechanistic explanation of the evolutionary process. It eliminates any need to invoke metaphysical principles for the origin of novelties in the evolutionary process.[10]

The phenomenon of emergence is therefore not mystical. But how consciousness actually emerges from the brain's internal flux does remain a complete mystery, and whether it will ever be solved is a matter of active debate among concerned scientists and philosophers.

A New Age of Discovery

We live not at the end of discovery but at the end of Reductionism, a time in which the false ideology of human mastery of all things through microscopics is being swept away by events and reason. This is not to say that microscopic law is wrong or has no purpose, but only that it is rendered irrelevant in many circumstances by its children and its children's children, the higher organizational laws of the world.[11]

—ROBERT B. LAUGHLIN, PROFESSOR OF PHYSICS,
STANFORD UNIVERSITY

---

9. Mayr, *Growth of Biological Thought*, 63.

10. Mayr, *What Makes Biology Unique?* 76–77.

11. Laughlin, *A Different Universe*, 221.

It Would Be Arrogant to Believe
Evolution Stops with Us

Charles Darwin's *The Origin of Species*, which describes biological evolution, was published first in 1859, with his final alterations in 1878. Darwin concludes his book with these words: "There is grandeur in this view of life, with its several powers, having been originally breathed by the Creator into a few forms or into one; and that, whilst this planet has gone cycling on according to the fixed law of gravity, from so simple a beginning endless forms most beautiful and most wonderful have been, and are being evolved."[12]

We tend to forget that Darwin's explanation, "endless forms . . . are being evolved," includes us—humanity. Freud's associate, Alfred Adler, also remarks upon the human tendency to be unaware of our existence on a larger scale: "We are in the midst of the stream of evolution, but we notice this as little as we do the spinning of the earth on its axis."[13]

Adler's observation also correctly notes that we are not at the pinnacle of evolution; indeed, it would be astonishingly arrogant to assume that after approximately 3.6 billion years since the beginning of primitive life forms, evolution suddenly stops with us.

So, as it continues, what is the target of evolution's selection? In other words, what is it about humanity that seeks to survive?

Mayr tells us that it is the individual as a whole. A small number of biologists, most publicly Richard Dawkins in England, have denied this. In his widely read books, beginning with *The Selfish Gene*,[14] Dawkins claims it is the survival of the gene that is fundamental, even to the detriment of the host individual. His books, well written in a popular style, have become influential in spreading this theme. But Ernst Mayr, whom many consider to be the leader in the field of theoretical biology, says,

> The idea that a few people have about the gene being the target of selection is completely impractical; a gene is never visible to natural selection. . . . Therefore people like Dawkins in England who still think the gene is the target of selection are evidently wrong. In the 30's and 40's, it was widely accepted that genes were the target of selection, because that was the only way they could be made

12. Darwin, *Origin of Species*, 560.
13. Adler, *Social Interest*, 109.
14. Dawkins, *The Selfish Gene*.

accessible to mathematics, but now we know that it is really the whole genotype of the individual, not the gene.[15]

British research biologist Steven Rose remarks, "Evolution continues, and is accelerating among humankind because of the products of human thought bringing about the accelerating interrelation of human minds. If the interrelated neurons of the human brain bring about consciousness, what will the quickening interrelation of human minds bring about?"[16]

The Evolutionary Step beyond the Human Mind

We know that 100 billion neurons in the brain, working in harmony with its other elements, produce the human mind. The human mind is tremendously more complex than the individual neurons that make it up. It is therefore capable of entering into even more complex interrelationships with other minds than the neuron is with other neurons.

Into what would billions of interacting human minds—each with the ability to visually communicate with each other and capable of acting independently but in highly empathetic support of others—evolve?

We have already begun to build the physical means to make such interrelation possible. The Internet can enable people everywhere to work closer together in greater cooperation and with greater understanding of each other than ever before. Even now, at the small cost of a Web page, anyone can make his thoughts instantly available worldwide to millions of other thinkers.

And the reverse is certainly true: as you learn the thoughts of diverse others, your own thinking, which causes physical change in your own brain, will be modified—presumably for the better—as your knowledge and appreciation of other views widens. Harvard psychologist Stephen Kosslyn concurs: "Your mind may arise not simply from your own brain, but in part from the brains of other people."[17]

The Internet grows in size, intricacy, density, and capability at such a startling rate that we cannot foresee what it will become in thirty years, much less three thousand years from now. The prerequisites for the

15. Mayr interview, "What Evolution Is."
16. Rose, *Lifelines: Biology beyond Determinism.*
17. Kosslyn, "2005."

emergence of a mind higher than that of humans, with capabilities beyond our imagination, will eventually be met—it may even be inevitable, unless prevented by the refusal of humanity to enter into such willing (if not always loving) communion with each other.

Is Humanity Too Selfish to Live and Work with True Empathy?

A major question arises: Aren't humans basically selfish creatures? And related to that issue, how could billions of people ever succeed in working together, willingly and harmoniously? Wouldn't the whole enterprise fall apart as a result of personal ambition, quarreling, jealousy, and war when tensions get too great? The Hebrew Lord in the books of Genesis and Exodus threatens—more than once—to destroy the human race, because its interactions are so evil. Nevertheless, there is reason for optimism.

Mayr, often referred to as the grand old man of evolutionary biology (he died in 2005 at the age of one hundred), was once asked, "How can the evolution of human ethics be reconciled with Darwinism? Doesn't natural selection always favor Darwinism?" He replied as follows:

> If the individual were the only target of selection, this would be an inevitable conclusion. However, small groups that compete with each other, such as the group of hunter-gatherers in our human ancestry, were, as groups, also targets of selection. Groups, the members of which actively cooperated with each other and showed much reciprocal helpfulness, have a higher chance for survival than groups that did not benefit from such cooperation and altruism. Any genetic tendency for altruism would therefore be selected in a species consisting of social groups. In a social group, altruism may add to the fitness. The founders of religions and philosophies erected their ethical systems on this basis.[18]

The greatly increased knowledge of and ability to communicate with other people via the Internet provides further reason for optimism: altruism. For example, the amount of compassion that individuals show is often a function of the closeness—in distance or similarity or relation—they feel to others.[19] In other words, you are much more likely to help a person you

18. Mayr interview, "What Evolution Is."

19. Editor's note: While there is much data on the correlation between closeness and altruistic behavior, Cialdini et al. (1997), contemporary of the author, also found

know or with whom you sympathize than someone with whom you feel nothing or whom you have never met.

Yet it is not necessary to be altruistic to do good; so it is not always easy to distinguish altruistic from nonaltruistic behavior. The monk who toils to help the poverty-stricken for the sole purpose of getting himself into heaven is doing good but not being altruistic. Nevertheless, the good he has done encourages closer human interrelations, itself a benefit greater than his initial good deed, thus helping humanity as well as the individuals involved.

In so helping humanity, people help themselves. This has been known for centuries in most religions but only more recently scientifically demonstrated in the social sciences: people often are happier when they help others, even putting the needs of others ahead of their own. In 1814, Thomas Jefferson wrote, "These good acts give pleasure, but how it happens that they give us pleasure? Because nature hath implanted in our breasts a love of others, a sense of duty to them, a moral instinct, in short, which prompts us irresistibly to feel and to succor their distresses."[20]

Perhaps if this truth were better advertised, more people (not necessarily religious) would become altruistic, as a purely selfish act!

Robert Axelrod, a political scientist at the University of Michigan, provided another reason—a surprising one—some years ago. Evolution is characterized by a competitive struggle for survival. Yet Axelrod mathematically showed (via clever computer simulation) that there is an evolutionary thrust for cooperation (*not* competition) that will, in his words, "emerge in a world of egoists without central authority."[21] The predictably irreverent Richard Dawkins remarked on Axelrod's book, "The world's leaders should all be locked up with this book and not released until they have read it. This would be a pleasure to them and might save the rest of us. *The Evolution of Cooperation* deserves to replace the Gideon Bible."[22]

The case for natural evolution resulting from cooperation rather than combat has also been made by one surprising source, Russian nobleman-turned revolutionary anarchist, Peter Kropotkin, who wrote *Mutual Aid* in

---

significant relation between a person's sense of "oneness" (i.e., merging of the self and other) and selfless activities. I believe this notion of "oneness" would have interested Bob, and perhaps it contributed to his thesis about man's sense of self in this work.

20. Quoted by Shermer, "Macroscope: The Soul of Science."

21. Axelrod, *The Evolution of Cooperation*.

22. Dawkins, "Preface," in Axelrod, *The Evolution of Cooperation*, x.

1902.[23] Evolutionary biologist Stephen Jay Gould concurs: "Kropotkin argues, in his cardinal premise, that the struggle for existence usually leads to mutual aid rather than combat as the chief criterion of evolutionary success. Human society must therefore build on our natural inclinations . . . in formulating a moral order that will bring both peace and prosperity to our species."[24]

Unfortunately, however, human beings are not only selfish; some can be criminal, perverted, fanatic, or insane. Since progress in science and technology, which includes the Internet, has shown itself to be easily disrupted, the harm such people can do is magnified, potentially extending to the endangerment of all civilization. In our own time, for example, we worry that nuclear and biological weapons that kill masses of people will fall (and have fallen) into the hands of terrorists. Yet neither the act of worrying nor the actions of a few extremists can halt the evolution of a species. As humanity has demonstrated, when new problems arise, so increases our capacity to solve them.

Thus, let us assume that humanity will one day learn to contain these problems within reasonable limits; to ensure our survival, we must. Very likely, we will have been enabled, in part, by what the Internet ideally becomes. It will have been an agent of change that both threatens our way of life and engenders our evolution beyond mere cooperation between peoples, towards a more comprehensive, intimate relationship between minds that truly understand each other.

Evolution proceeds inexorably, with discrete jumps in an organism's state of being. Each higher state allows the organism to emerge as a new whole, with characteristics significantly different from the one below, but more importantly, as a new entity interacting differently with other entities and with its environment.

As humanity rises to these higher states, over the eons we periodically stop to reflect upon and even muse as to what the next level will look like: How will people appear? What will communication between people involve? And once we achieve true understanding of each other, what will be the next jump, beyond the level of the mind? Is there going to be a step in our evolution that unites human self-awarenesses? If so, how can we even describe (and comprehend) what that emerged state would be?

My understanding of an emerged state of self-awareness is that it consists of a unique superconsciousness with qualities so much deeper and

23. P. Kropotkin, *Mutual Aid*.

24. Gould, "Kropotkin Was No Crackpot," 12–21.

richer than our own that it remains beyond our human senses to detect or our mental ability to conceive.

A Theoretical Physicist's Concept of God

Like the majority of scientists in this century, I have not concerned myself seriously with theology. Theology is a foreign language which we have not taken the trouble to learn. . . .

I do not make any clear distinction between mind and God. God is what mind becomes when it has passed beyond the scale of our comprehension.[25]

—FREEMAN DYSON, INSTITUTE FOR ADVANCED STUDY, PRINCETON

A Richer Selfness beyond the Self

What would be the properties of the superconsciousness, the higher level of being emerged from the loving union of human self-awarenesses?

The highest biological whole of which we know, that of human being, has the capacity to maintain stability by adjusting for and repairing certain internal failures.[26] Neurologist Oliver Sacks writes, "It must be said . . . that a disease is never a mere loss or excess, that there is always a reaction, on the part of the affected organism or individual, to restore, to replace, to compensate for and to preserve its identity."[27]

A human body whose skin gets scratched, for example, will quickly repair it. Surgeon Sherwin B. Nuland explains:

> The central nervous system consists of the brain and spinal cord, while the peripheral nervous system consists of the nerves that carry messages into and out of the brain and cord, traveling to and from the internal tissues and periphery of the body. . . . These [peripheral system] receiving structures are located in the skin, muscle, and the various internal organs and are attuned to events happening in both the outside world and the inner world of the body's constant

---

25. Dyson, *Infinite in All Directions*, 119.

26. Maturana and Varela, *Autopoiesis and Cognition*. This is a pioneering book opening up new lines of thought in complexity study.

27. Sacks, *Man Who Mistook His Wife for a Hat*.

functioning. When the brain and cord have processed the information thus brought to them, they send their responses back to the body via outgoing nerves of the peripheral system.[28]

Nuland then exults, "I do not hesitate to propose that man is in some as-yet-undiscovered way more than the sum of his biological parts, that a thing greater than the innate has somehow been crafted from the innate."[29] The mindful man, says Nuland, has emerged from human-body-with-brain, in some unknown way, at a higher level of being than the components that make him up.

Consider what Nuland's words mean if evolutionary change continues beyond the stage of our selves. The human-body-with-brain tries to restore its wholeness when part of itself fails. Oftentimes it succeeds, such as when mending a fractured bone, by sending appropriate signals to appropriate organs. Correspondingly, a superconsciousness that evolves into a unity from the minds of humanity would try to repair a part of itself that fails—in this case a human mind—in order to make itself whole again.

Since this relation of the emergent whole to its individual components takes place on a level far beyond our experience, we cannot yet picture it. We know only that, as each evolutionary step has shown in the past, a richer, fuller relationship results than that which occurred on the preceding lower level of being.

This is ordinary inductive reasoning, not theology.

To Be or Not to Be

A central question is whether humanity can ever act compassionately enough, empathetically enough, lovingly enough for that evolutionary leap to take place, even in the extremely faraway future.

By first reflecting historically, we realize that the earliest *Homo sapiens* appeared only about 200,000 years ago. Earth is estimated to be 4.5 to 5 billion years old; in other words, it existed for over 4 billion years before anatomically modern man evolved. Yet we, today, have evolved very differently—both physically and mentally—from those first humans. So it is clear that 200,000 years is a relatively short time in the history of the planet, and we cannot possibly imagine what humankind will be like (if

28. Nuland, *Wisdom of the Body*, 75–76.
29. Nuland, *Wisdom of the Body*, 68.

humanity lasts) or what technological advances will exist another 200,000 years from now.

Left only to speculation, then, we can but imagine that the intricate relationship between individuals on an Internet-like network will have grown from its primitive beginnings to a level of complexity great enough to produce emergent behavior. Hopefully, by then people will have learned to live in compassionate empathy for one another.

If so, there is a momentous corollary. Einstein's theories have shown that there is no boundary separating past, present, and future in the physical world. Past and future are both as real as the present. However, an aspect of our own consciousness narrows our awareness of what we consider to be the present.

It follows that, *if at some time in the distant future, a unity representing superconsciousness—that is, superselfness—emerges from human selves, then, I posit, there will exist, as there existed before and now exists, the evolutionary God who is that superconsciousness.*

The Last Judgment of Humanity

Lev Shestov, one of the founders of modern existentialism, was a Russian Jewish thinker who emigrated to France after the Bolshevik revolution. In 1922, he became professor of Russian philosophy at the University of Paris. In 1929, he wrote,

> The Last Judgment is the supreme reality. In moments—their rare moments—of illumination, even our positive thinkers feel this. . . . And maybe, even the existence of God is still undecided. Even God waits, like every living human soul, on the Last Judgment.
>
> A great battle is going on, a battle between life and death, between real and ideal, and we men do not even guess what is happening in the universe, and are deeply convinced that we need not know, as though it did not matter to us![30]

Shestov's "Last Judgment" can be seen as a metaphor for humanity's ultimate decision: Will we act together in such a manner that the evolutionary step beyond humanity to God eventually takes place?

---

30. Shestov, *Na vesakh Iova*, 145. Quoted by Kuvakin, *History of Russian Philosophy*, 609.

9

The Hebrew Lord

A RUMBLING: Truth itself has appeared among humankind in the
very thick of their flurrying metaphors.

—PAUL CELAN[1]

The Hebrew Lord and the
Evolutionary God

I BELIEVE THAT THE evolutionary God, who emerges from a distant future
era in which humanity has achieved harmony and goodness, *is* the Hebrew
Lord of biblical times. Furthermore, as understood in this scientific age,
He would emerge from all humanity, not only from descendants of the
ancient Israelites.[2]

So how can the two be perceived as the same God?

In the Hebrew Bible, the covenant between God and the Israelites is the
fundamental relationship between them. To keep the covenant, to keep the
Hebrew Lord as their God, people must also keep the law of Moses and act
morally and charitably with one another. In the First Book of Kings, when
the people did not do so, but acted evilly, the Hebrew Lord did not appear to
them. Likewise, the evolutionary God does not emerge unless people empathize, live lovingly with each other, and care for those in need.

The Hebrew Lord tells us through the prophet Isaiah that He prefers
that people act in this manner over praying to Him; this is biblical law.

---

1. Celan, *Atemwende*. Translated from the German by Michael Hamburger. Ac-
claimed poet Celan survived a concentration camp where his parents perished. He lived
in Paris after the war, but amidst his success he drowned himself in the Seine at age
forty-nine.

2. This result from the Hebrew Bible differs from that in the New Testament, in
which the second coming of Jesus brings the end of this world and its replacement by a
spiritual-like realm.

The evolutionary God can exist only if people act in this manner; this is natural law. In each understanding, the Lord both transcends the world and is immanent. In other words, He is simultaneously not of this world, yet part of everything that defines it.

In a similar way, an individual's consciousness of self, the feeling of "I am," underlies the human understanding of the Hebrew Lord, YHWH, who had instructed Moses to tell the people that His name means "I AM."[3] As for the evolutionary God, He will one day emerge from the human self-consciousness—that is, from the *union* of each person's "I am."

In either the evolutionary or biblical view, our comprehension of the Lord is limited to His involvement with humanity. Neither science nor the Bible permits us to say anything else about the nature of God. We must therefore limit ourselves to theorizing that the creation of the evolutionary God by emergence from humankind in the distant future is an event that may be predictable by inductive reasoning, but its method of accomplishment remains a great mystery.

Emergence, though a known phenomenon, cannot be satisfactorily explained by theoretical biologists. This does not mean that it has no rational explanation, only that present-day science has not yet achieved its understanding.[4] Hopefully, that understanding is also still evolving.

The (Big) Fly in the Ointment

But there are aspects of the Hebrew Lord that do not fit into this epiphany: his apparent capriciousness and sometime cruelty. In the Bible's narrative portions, the Hebrew Lord often acts arbitrarily, angrily, harshly—at times too cruel to be palatable to the modern mind. The always-sober evolutionary God never acts in such ways.

An instance is the biblical God's response to the Israelites who had fled from Egypt under Moses and were camped on the plains of Moab, where they mixed with the Moabites, bowing down to the Moabite gods, their men fornicating with Moabite women: "And YHWH said to Moses,

---

3. Exodus 3:14. Friedman, *Commentary on the Torah.*

4. It is here that proponents of an unfortunately widespread movement in the United States, "Intelligent Design," err in jumping to the conclusion that that which we do not understand must be the work of a superior intelligence—an intelligence that they identify with God.

'Take all of the leaders of the people and hang them in front of the sun, and YHWH's flaring anger will go back from Israel.'"[5]

The story tells us that 24,000 were killed. YHWH then instructs Moses to "Get revenge for the children of Israel from the Midianites."[6] So the Israelites burn down Midianite cities, slaughtering every male and every woman who is not a virgin, but keeping the virginal women for themselves.

The stated motivation for such ugly acts was the preservation of the Israelite people and their way of worshipping YHWH. Israelites identified YHWH as only *their* God—not the God of other peoples. Today, Jews, Christians, and Muslims consider YHWH to be the one God of all humanity, and such slaughter would be considered an unjustifiable horror.

When the Israelites were in the desert of Sinai, they crafted an idol for worship while Moses was with God on the mountain. God, angry, told Moses he wanted to save him but destroy the Israelites and start over. But Moses, who would have made an excellent used car salesman, talked God out of it by using psychology—by saying it would shame him in the eyes of the Egyptians:

> And YHWH said to Moses, "I've seen this people; and here, it's a hard-necked people. And now leave off from me, and my anger will flare at them, and I'll finish them, and I'll make you into a big nation!"
>
> And Moses conciliated in front of YHWH, his God, and said, "Why, YHWH, should your anger flare at your people whom you brought out from the land of Egypt with big power and with a strong hand? Why should Egypt say, saying, 'He brought them out for bad, to kill them in the mountains, and to finish them from on the face of the earth'? Turn back from your flaring anger, and relent about the bad to your people." . . .
>
> And YHWH relented about the bad that He had spoken to do to his people.[7]

The Hebrew Bible is a human record of writings and memories compiled over a thousand years—from about 1200 BCE to 200 BCE—which tells of Israel's struggle to understand and do the will of God. Biblical stories have been told, retold, told again, and recorded by imperfect human beings. In them, the Hebrew Lord's actions do not always seem godly; in fact, they

---

5. Numbers 25:4. Friedman, *Commentary on the Torah.*

6. Numbers 31:2. Friedman, *Commentary on the Torah.*

7. Exodus 32:9–12. Friedman, *Commentary on the Torah.*

often seem too human. He is sometimes savage, angry, regretful for what he has done; sometimes He changes His mind and is willing to debate—or even lose to human beings.

So biblical stories must be understood in that manner: the telling of the struggle of a God-obsessed people to do the will of their God as they perceive it, even to the extent of trying occasionally to change His will.

After Israel's trials and tribulations, the Hebrew Lord Who finally emerges in the prophetic writings is all good, all compassionate. He thus corresponds to an evolutionary God with the dominant characteristic of caring for His people, while lesser traits, such as revenge, fade away. Likewise, we will continue our own Darwinian evolution, ideally with enough compassionate empathy as good and loving individuals to develop into a unity that represents the also-evolving, interconnected, collective consciousness of humanity.

The Hebrew Lord as Teacher

The progressive disclosure of God's attitude towards humanity in the Bible—from the primitive one in the book of Genesis to the elevated one in the books of the prophets—is also the description of a good teacher.

The Bible tells of the gradual withdrawing of God from human contact, growing more remote while at the same time demanding more from human beings.

In God's first encounter with humans, He interacts with them in a direct and personal way: God walks with Adam and Eve in the cool of the day; He asks them directly not to eat from the tree of knowledge and chats with them, while they, like young children, try to hide from Him.

God continues this sort of intimate interaction when He walks with Noah, giving him direction to build and occupy an ark with a male and female from every type of life.

When God communicates with Abraham, the conversations are often through messengers and angels. Rather than "walking" with humans as He had with Adam and Eve, God enjoins Abraham to leave home and start a worshipful life anew. Abraham hears the voice of God, though he does not see Him. God talks to Moses no longer as a person, but rather from the burning bush or mountaintop, as only God could, instructing him to lead the people out of Egypt. In the wilderness, God speaks from a pillar of cloud on the mountain so people can hear but not see Him as He delivers His law to

Moses. God's presence is perceived by the people, but only in a cloud. In the last book of the Torah, Deuteronomy, it is Moses alone who retells the history to the people and reminds them of their covenant with God.[8]

Finally, then, the biblical narrative leads to the full withdrawal of the Hebrew Lord from direct contact with humanity, His words transmitted only through the mouths of great prophets. God's withdrawal culminates in His most difficult demand of all, a demand on the people as a whole: do the will of God in the ways you treat others.[9] This, YHWH says through the prophets, is the proper way to worship Him. The prophet Isaiah then enlarges the vision to include not just the Israelites and their descendants but all the peoples of the world: "For My House shall be called a house of prayer for all peoples."[10]

In the Bible, then, God acts like a teacher. For example, in kindergarten, a teacher sits down with the children, talks, and plays with them. As they grow older, she gives them instruction so they can work together and moves occasionally among them to guide and help. In high school, she stands in front of the class as she talks, now separated from its members. In college she may find herself lecturing in a large hall, not knowing most of the students by name. Increasingly in universities, in fact, she does not see the students at all, nor they her. She is a disembodied presence, sometimes represented online as an image or voice through a computer, sometimes as a simple photograph or drawing, and sometimes she has no representation at all. At each higher level of instruction, as the teacher withdraws, more is required from the student.

I believe this analogy parallels the stages of the evolutionary God, who is also YHWH, the Lord of the Hebrew Bible. So if God acts as a teacher, and the emergent God is also the Hebrew Lord, what will become of people's relationship to God if the Israelites or their descendants mess up?

A Precarious Relationship

In the Bible, God has Moses tell the Israelites that, to them, His name, YHWH, means, "I AM."[11] If they obey His law, it is by being "I AM" that the Lord will

8. Deuteronomy 1:3. Friedman, *Commentary on the Torah.*

9. For an insightful discussion of the gradual withdrawal of God from the Bible and the people, see Friedman, *Hidden Face of God.*

10. Isaiah 56:7. JPS.

11. Exodus 3:14. Friedman, *Commentary on the Torah.*

relate to the "I am" of each Israelite. The Lord, speaking to the people through Moses, said, "And now, if you'll *listen* to my voice and observe my covenant, then you'll be a treasure to me out of all the peoples, because all the earth is mine. And you'll be a kingdom of priests and a holy nation to me."[12]

Here the similarity of the Hebrew Lord to the evolutionary God is clear. It is keeping the covenant and following the precepts revealed through Moses that comprise the guide to living life in an ethical way, which in turn leads to the emerging unity of all people.

But what if the Hebrews act wrongfully and do not keep the covenant with YHWH? Speaking through Hosea, God tells the people that, because they have behaved wickedly, the Hebrew Lord no longer exists for them:

> For you are not my people,
> and I will not be your [God].[13]

No, a word has not been left out of the second line. The Jewish Publication Society's new biblical translation assumes that an important word has been left out and renders that second line, "and I will not be your [God]."

Other English versions freely add the word "God" or similarly imply it belongs there. But these translations are distortions of the Hebrew that miss the theological doctrine being expressed. The Hebrew for "be" in the biblical passage means "to exist."[14] *God is literally saying that he no longer exists as I AM for the Hebrews when they behave wickedly.*

God's words are in accord with evolutionary biology's thesis that a higher level of existence emerges only from an appropriate unity of elements on the level just below.

When God Is

So you are My witnesses—declares the Lord [YHWH]—
And I am God.[15]

If you are my witnesses, then I am God,
But if you are not my witnesses, then I am, as it were, not God.[16]

---

12. Exodus 19:5–6. Friedman, *Commentary on the Torah.*
13. Hosea 1:8–9. JPS.
14. For more, see Plastaras, *The God of Exodus*, 98.
15. Isaiah 43:12. JPS.
16. Adapted from Kahana, Babylonian Talmud.

Can a Person Feel the Presence of God?

Accordingly, when a person acts generously, altruistically, lovingly, or performs deeds that help bring about progress toward the perfection of human society, he is therefore doing the will of the evolutionary God. When, in 2005, the more prosperous nations of the world responded to a great natural disaster—the tsunami that devastated Southeast Asia—with an instinctive outpouring of sympathy and aid to the victims, they were doing the will of God. Though the participants were not able to feel the actual presence of God, presumably they were able to feel that they were doing His will, which is, at least, akin to feeling His presence.

A mainstay of mysticism is the belief that people can sometimes feel the presence of God. Sigmund Freud (no mystic, he) has written of "the oceanic feeling," which, he says, is one he himself had never experienced. Romain Rolland, famed author of *Jean-Christophe* and many other works including two on Hindu mystics, had sent Freud a letter concerning Freud's recent book that claimed religion is an illusion. Freud writes of that letter,

> He [Rolland] was sorry I had not properly appreciated the true source of religious sentiments. This, he says, consists in a peculiar feeling, which he himself is never without, which he finds confirmed by many others, and which he may suppose is present in millions of people. It is a feeling which he would like to call a sensation of "eternity," a feeling as of something limitless, unbounded—as it were "oceanic." This feeling, he adds, is a purely subjective fact, not an article of faith; it brings with it no assurance of personal immortality, but it is the source of the religious energy which is seized upon by the various Churches and religious systems.[17]

Both Rolland and Freud accepted this "oceanic feeling" as real but rejected the idea that it indicates the presence of God. Rolland agreed with Freud that religion is illusion.

One of today's foremost research neurologists, V. S. Ramachandran,[18] has noted that in seizures in the limbic system of the brain, some patients have "deeply moving spiritual experiences, including a feeling of divine presence and the sense that they are in direct communion with God." Ramachandran writes, "I find it ironic that this sense of enlightenment,

17. Freud, *Civilization and Its Discontents*, 11–12.

18. V. S. Ramachandran is professor and director of the Center for Brain and Cognition, University of California, San Diego, and adjunct professor at the Salk Institute for Biological Studies in La Jolla.

this absolute conviction that Truth is revealed at last, should derive from limbic structures concerned with emotions rather than from the thinking, rational parts of the brain that take so much pride in their ability to discern truth and falsehood."[19]

Do these words carry a valuable lesson in humility?

Ramachandran says that, from his and other neurologists' observations, "the one clear conclusion that emerges . . . is that there are circuits in the human brain that are involved in religious experience and these become hyperactive in some epileptics."[20] In some documented cases, these experiences have led to religious conversion.[21] He further speculates: "Could it be that human beings have actually evolved specialized neural circuitry for the sole purpose of mediating religious experience? The human belief in the supernatural is so widespread in all societies all over the world that it's tempting to ask whether the propensity for such beliefs has a biological basis. If so, you'd have to answer a key question: What sorts of Darwinian selection pressures could lead to such a mechanism?"[22]

It is also possible that these phenomena have nothing to do either with God or true religion—that they are only products of the human mind and are magnified in some epileptics. Perhaps the antireligious, antimystical Sigmund Freud was right when he rejected the oceanic feeling as not meaningful. The evolutionary Lord of the Hebrew Bible demands not an oceanic feeling but contribution to the perfecting of humanity, including concern and care for those in most need. On the other hand, can such concern be precursor to or the result of an "oceanic feeling?"

The jury is out.

The Embarrassment of Being "Chosen"

While still in the Sinai desert, Moses tells the Israelites, "Because you are a holy people to YHWH, your God, YHWH, your God, chose you to become a treasured people to Him out of all the peoples who are on the face of the earth."[23]

19. Ramachandran and Blakeslee, *Phantoms in the Brain*, 179.

20. Ramachandran and Blakeslee, *Phantoms in the Brain*, 188.

21. Ramachandran and Blakeslee, *Phantoms in the Brain*, 285.

22. Ramachandran and Blakeslee, *Phantoms in the Brain*, 183.

23. Deuteronomy 7:6. Friedman, *Commentary on the Torah*.

Why did the biblical God choose the children of Israel? We are not sure of the origin of the little ditty, "How odd of God to choose the Jews." But we do know it arose in England, where a genteel anti-Semitism has been endemic in aristocratic and intellectual circles. Its classic rejoinder is, "Though not so odd as those who choose a Jewish God and spurn the Jews."[24]

In today's democratic age, we—Jew and non-Jew alike—are prone to downplay the idea of being chosen by God, ascribing it to primitive biblical thinking. Many peoples' stories of their origins include ideas of being in some fashion special to their gods. But unfortunately, in this instance, for the Jewish people, the holy book of the Jews has been chosen as a component of an aggressive and much larger religion.

Some synagogues have eliminated from their ritual any reference to being chosen.[25] But the theme continued to be influential throughout the centuries during which the Bible was composed. Toward the end of that period, the prophet whose name we do not know, but whom we call "Second Isaiah," uncompromisingly confirms, "'My witnesses are *you'*—declares the Lord [YHWH]—'My servant whom I have chosen.'"[26] Clearly, it is an important idea in biblical thought.

A Talmudic fable says that God offered the Torah to all the peoples on earth, and only the Israelites were willing to live the way it prescribes and accept it. But this is not so according to the Hebrew Bible: as the Bible makes clear again and again, God thinks of the Jews as a stubborn, stiff-necked, obstinate people who resisted being chosen.[27]

In the book of Deuteronomy, for example, Moses tells the Hebrews, "So you shall know that it is not because of your virtue that YHWH, your God, gives you this good land to take possession of it, for you are a hard-necked people."[28]

As a Jew, I can confirm that we still are. But why did the biblical Lord pick such a difficult people? Of all those available to Him, why on earth did God choose the Jews?

24. Quoted by Wouk in *This Is My God*, 30.

25. The Reconstructionist movement in Conservative Judaism has removed the concept of being chosen from their prayer book.

26. Isaiah 43:10. JPS.

27. See Exodus 32:9, 33:3, 33:5, 34:9; Deuteronomy 9:6, 9:13, 9:27, 10:16; Hosea 4:16; Ezekiel 3:7; Isaiah 62:1–5.

28. Deuteronomy 9:6. Friedman, *Commentary on the Torah*.

Spinoza, who had answers for most theological questions, was confused by this one—he had two conflicting answers within the same chapter of the same book. He says that telling the Israelites they were a chosen people was a strategy on the part of Moses: "Moses wished to admonish the Jews in a particular way, using such reasoning as would bind them more firmly to the worship of God, having regard to the immaturity of their understanding."[29]

Two pages later he writes, "The Hebrew nation was chosen by God before all others not by reason of its understanding nor of its spiritual qualities, but by reason of its social organization and the good fortune whereby it achieved supremacy and retained it for so many years."[30]

Neither answer could be called complimentary, and the latter seems rather far fetched, considering the tumultuous history of the ancient Hebrew nations, Israel and Judah. In his writings, Spinoza resisted giving the Jews credit for anything of a positive nature. It may have been because of bitterness remaining after his excommunication; or it may have been part of the guise through which he presented his beliefs to an intolerant world. But the theme of the chosen people is too strong in the Bible to let the thought of an embittered Spinoza be decisive.

29. Spinoza, *Tractatus Theologico-Politicus*, 89.
30. Spinoza, *Tractatus Theologico-Politicus*, 91.

The Eternal Riddle

Israel, my people,
God's greatest riddle,
Will thy solution
Ever be told

Fought—never conquered,
Bent—never broken,
Mortal—immortal,
Youthful, though old.

Egypt enslaved thee,
Babylon crushed thee,
Rome led thee captive,
Homeless thy head.

Where are those nations
Mighty and fearsome
Thou hast survived them,
They are long dead.

Nations keep coming,
Nations keep going,
Passing like shadows,
Wiped off the earth.

Thou an eternal
Witness remainest,
Watching their burial,
Watching their birth.

Pray, who revealed thee
Heaven's great secret :
Death and destruction,
Thus to defy

Suffering torture,
Stake, inquisition—
Prithee, who taught thee
Never to die

Ay, and who gave thee
Faith, deep as ocean,
Strong as the rock-hills,
Fierce as the sun

Hated and hunted,
Ever thou wand'rest,
Bearing a message:
God is but one!

Pray, has thy saga
Likewise an ending,
As its beginning
Glorious of old

Israel, my people,
God's greatest riddle,
Will thy solution
Ever be told

—P. M. RASKIN[31]

31. Raskin, *Book of Jewish Thoughts.*

Another possible explanation that should have appealed to Spinoza and follows from the words of God and Moses is that the ancient Hebrews and consequently the Jews descended from them are a willful, stubborn people—too obstinate to succumb to the hardship, ostracism, and persecution to which they would be subjected; too obstinate to give in to the blandishments and enticement of escape from reality that other religions offer.

For over two thousand years, inducement and death threats have not succeeded in weaning the Jews away from their biblical heritage, their belief that it is their duty, in Isaiah's words, to be "a light of nations"[32] and so to hasten the coming of a golden age of peace on earth.

"I Am a Tibetan Jew! I Am a Tibetan Jew!"

The survival of the Jews is not an easy act for others to follow.

Tibet's Dalai Lama has been exiled by China from his own country since 1959, now making his headquarters in the village of Dharamsala in northern India. Concerned about his own people's cultural survival outside Tibet, he has consulted Jewish groups on how Jews have been able to survive without a country for thousands of years.[33] During a visit to the United States in 1989, he requested a meeting with representatives of the four major branches of Judaism, Orthodox, Reform, Conservative and Reconstructionist. He wanted to learn the "Jewish 'secret technique' of survival," which for him was a practical and not academic question. On another occasion, the Dalai Lama, who is open, friendly, and laughs easily with all people, put on a Jewish skullcap given him as a gift and walked about chuckling, "I am a Tibetan Jew! I am a Tibetan Jew!"[34]

32. Isaiah 49:6. JPS.

33. Commentator: "Dalai Lama Meets Jews from 4 Major Branches," New York Times Archives, 1989. https://nyti.ms/29ylQYc.

34. Reported by Gil Kopateh in *Haaretz Magazine* (June 3, 2005), 18–21.

God's Inheritance

The Hebrew Bible often refers to Israel as God's "inheritance."[35] For example, in the book of Deuteronomy, Moses entreats God not to punish Israel for its wickedness: "And I prayed to YHWH, and said, 'My Lord YHWH, don't destroy your people and your legacy. . . . They're your people and your legacy.'"[36] The prophet, Jeremiah, says of God, "For He is the One Who formed everything. And Israel is the tribe of his inheritance."[37]

These passages raise an intriguing question: From whom could God, creator of all according to Jeremiah, possibly have inherited Israel? We cannot put ourselves in the minds of ancient Hebrews to determine the undeclared assumptions of their thought, but the evolutionary approach provides one possible answer: God inherited Israel from Israel itself! Through its biblical prophets, Israel has lit the way for the nations of the world to eventually unite in a golden age from which God could emerge.

Such an apparent paradox is not troubling, however, in a world where time does not necessarily flow evenly for everyone. Today's world, with an understanding of Einstein's special relativity,[38] opens us to the possibility of a relationship in which each cause and each effect supports and strengthens the other. Indeed, it may not be a paradox at all but perhaps the only explanation.

In Summary

In the Bible, the Hebrew Lord's intrinsic nature is beyond human understanding. The prophet Isaiah quotes God as follows:

> "For My thoughts are not your thoughts,
>
> Nor are your ways My ways," declares the Lord [YHWH].
>
> "For as the heavens are higher than the earth,
>
> So are My ways higher than your ways,
>
> And My thoughts than your thoughts."[39]

35. See discussion in Kluger, *Psyche and Bible*, 13–15. Kluger, a collaborator of Carl Jung, advised Jung on biblical matters.

36. Deuteronomy 9:26, 29. Friedman, *Commentary on the Torah*.

37. Jeremiah 10:16. Chabad.org.

38. Editor's note: See Einstein's "Twin Paradox" and other theoretical time travel experiments, where, according to Russian physicist Igor Novikov, probability can bend to prevent a paradox.

39. Isaiah 55:8. NASB.

Biblical Hebrew is a concrete language, and abstractions, such as thoughts, are presented in concrete terms. God told Moses that He, God, whose name, YHWH, means to the people "I AM," is also "I AM" on a higher level of being. Therefore, the Hebrew Lord relates to people by being inclusive of the lesser "I am's" of you and me. But even as we do today, the people often did not listen to God's voice from within:

> I said, "Here am I, here am I,"
> To a nation which did not call on My name.[40]

This is God in search of man, who is not always willing to be found, said Abraham Joshua Heschel.[41]

Just as the human body maintains its living unity by concern for and repair to minor injuries of individual parts, so does the Hebrew Lord, the Supreme Self, maintain His unimaginable higher unity by His concern for individual human selves.

In our understanding of biblical thought, then, the human self is not lost in God. There is, however, a common metaphor in many religions and their mystical aspects that God is like the ocean, and the individual human mind is a wave that loses itself within that ocean. But if we consider the hierarchical nature of an evolving reality, this is a false metaphor. The Hebrew Lord exists on a higher level than do the individual selves who unite to make Him up, but He also only exists because each human self maintains its own being—just as the human mind exists only because individual neurons and other elements that make it up maintain their own existence. Thus, the Hebrew Lord is concerned for each individual.

The Hebrew Lord as an evolutionary God therefore depends both upon His relationship with individuals and upon the ability of those individuals to unite in heeding His voice. The Bible limits itself to describing the individual and collective relationships between God and humans, but it does not attempt to teach every aspect of the Hebrew Lord. In fact, from the standpoint of the mystical system of Kabbalah, the Hebrew Lord is not the full God but rather an aspect of God—that which relates to humanity. The Kabbalah calls God's fullness *Ein Sof*[42]—that is, beyond human reach,

40. Isaiah 65:1.

41. Heschel, *God in Search of Man*. See, for example, 425, "Judaism Is God's Quest for Man."

42. "Kabbalah" is the term that describes aspects of Jewish mysticism. "*Ein Sof* is the name given in the Kabbalah to God transcendent, in His pure essence." Roth, *Encyclopedia Judaica*.

understanding, or comprehension. This is consistent with Spinoza's observation that God has an infinite number of attributes, of which we humans can apprehend only matter and mind—for now.

Life on Other Worlds?
A Far-Out Speculation

Will technological advancement some day in the distant future enable science to discover conscious selves elsewhere in the universe, also engaged in evolutionary striving towards the emergence of transcendent unity? It would be a unity of different selves in a different world leading to a different Name for God.

I realize what an understatement it would be to note the insuperable difficulty of discovering conscious selves elsewhere than on Earth: the state of today's knowledge is such that science hardly knows how to detect consciousness of self right here—even of you and me. Perhaps beings discovered on another planet would merely be program-following, self-reproducing robots originally created by a now extinct society—machines without consciousness.

But if we were able to make such a discovery—and much imagination is required here—then the one God of the extended universe may emerge through the complexities of interstellar communication from the unity of all his Names—two emergences above us (one from our own humanity on this earth and the other from the larger universe)—incomprehensible, unimaginable, ineffable: the *Ein Sof* of Kabbalah.

10

The Question of Evil Times

The NO with which the Jews, so dangerously over the centuries,
replied to the calls of the church, does not express an absurd stubbornness, but the conviction that important human truths in the
Old Testament were being lost in the theology of the New.

—EMMANUEL LEVINAS[1]

ELIE WIESEL, WHO SURVIVED confinement in a German concentration
camp, won the Nobel Prize for his writings about the Holocaust. In his
novel, *Night*, based on his personal experience, he tells of an execution of
three people in the camp, one a child, suspected of resistance: the three
victims mounted together onto the chairs. The three necks were placed at
the same moment within the nooses.

> "Long live liberty!" cried the two adults.
> But the child was silent.
> "Where is God? Where is He?" Someone behind me asked.
> At a sign from the head of the camp, the three chairs tipped
> over.
> Total silence throughout the camp. On the horizon the sun
> was setting.
> Then the march past began. The two adults were no longer
> alive. Their tongues hung swollen, blue tinged. But the third rope
> was still moving; being so light the child was still alive. . . .
> For more than half an hour he stayed there, struggling be-
> tween life and death, dying in slow agony under our eyes. And we
> had to look him full in the face. He was still alive when I passed in
> front of him. His tongue was still red, his eyes were not yet glazed.
> Behind me, I heard the same man asking:
> "Where is God now?"

1. Levinas, *Difficult Freedom*, 275. Levinas taught at the Sorbonne in Paris.

And I heard a voice behind me answer him:

"Where is He? Here He is—He is hanging here on this gallows."[2]

Wiesel was fifteen at the time of his internment; he was mystically inclined and had a deeply religious upbringing. He originally wrote the book in Yiddish, with the title, *Un di velt hut geshvign* (*And the World Remained Silent*). When the English version, *Night*, was released, however, his opening paragraph in Yiddish had been omitted from the translation. Here it is now:

> In the beginning there was faith, a naïve faith; and there was trust, a foolish trust; and there was illusion, a frightful illusion. We had faith in God, trust in man, and we were living an illusion. We pretended that a holy spark glowed in each of us; that the Divine image dwells in our soul and shines in our eyes. Alas, this was the source, if not the cause, of the misfortune that befell us.[3]

Wiesel, much like Job more than two thousand years earlier and like innumerable suffering persons since, discovered that, if he were still willing to believe in God, then *this* was not the God that fit the comfortable picture drawn by popular religion.

This was the evolutionary Lord, though He could not have prevented the hanging any more than He could have prevented the Nazi era. During that time, humanity was not yet morally advanced enough (nor is it now) for Him to act through it. He does act through humanity but remains unable to prevent great evil in our time.

The Self and Others

The name of God, the Bible tells us, culminating in the words of the prophets, demands that people relate to each other on a self-to-self basis: "Love your neighbor as yourself," says the Book of Leviticus. It is a relation of "I am" to another "I am" under the aegis of "I AM."

Modern interpreters of Judaism have put this in contemporary language. Martin Buber writes that each of us should treat another person as a "thou," as another conscious feeling self, and not as an "it"—an object for use. Emmanuel Levinas differentiates his view from what he calls

---

2. Wiesel, *Night*, 61–62.

3. Pfefferkorn and Hirsch, "Wiesel's Wrestle with God," 20.

Buber's reciprocal relationships, saying that we can encounter God through the face-to-face relationship with another human being, and that God's presence is encountered in meeting the need expressed in the face of the other person: "The word 'transcendence' precisely indicates that we cannot think, God, and be one. By the same token, in terms of interpersonal relationships, it is not about thinking of myself and the other as one, but rather about facing the other. The true union or togetherness is not one of synthesis, but rather one of being face to face."[4]

Albert Einstein writes, "What is the meaning of human life, or of organic life altogether? To answer this question at all implies a religion. Is there any sense then, you ask, in putting it? I answer, the man who regards his own life and that of his fellow creatures as meaningless is not merely unfortunate but almost disqualified for life."[5]

Loving relationships between human selves, between human minds, are necessary for that next great step in evolution to take place: God emerging from the uniting of humankind. The Hebrew Lord acts through the unity of human minds, meeting in loving embrace; the more extensive that embrace—that is, the more people acting in such a manner—the more extensive the Lord's ability to act.

It may then be reasonably claimed that there is no miracle in the Lord's actions. If people are loving enough to avoid doing evil, then evil things will not be done.

The prevention of great evil requires great human unity, though humanity, as we bitterly know, has not gotten far in reaching its ultimate goal. In times of great evil, the Hebrew Lord can only suffer with the suffering; He can only urge humanity to remember His Name, listen to the prophets, and act accordingly, because only then, when people will have evolved, can the golden age of universal love and contentment be attained.

Bringing about "the Messianic Age"

In postbiblical times, the early rabbis named the hoped-for golden era under God's rule the "Messianic Age," with the "Messiah" as its harbinger. The Talmud tells the story of Joshua ben Levi, who lived two thousand years ago in the land of Israel, at a time of great suffering under Roman siege. Joshua

4. Editor's note: Translated from Levinas, *Ethique et infini*, 72.

5. Editor's note: Einstein, *The World as I See It*, 1.

demanded to know when the Messiah would come, and he was given the answer: "Today, if only you will listen to God's voice."[6]

The phrasing has changed since then, but the message has not. For example, in the twentieth century, Abraham Joshua Heschel concluded a series of lectures on the nature of man at Stanford University, with the following admonition: "By whatever we do, by every act we carry out, we either advance or obstruct the drama of redemption; we either reduce or enhance the power of evil."[7]

Einstein, too, offers his view on the role that people must play in bringing about a golden era. He writes: "Whatever there is of God and goodness in the universe, it must work itself out and express itself through us. We cannot stand aside and let God do it.[8]

According to the Bible, this step to the Messianic Age can be achieved only if humanity can radically change its thinking. In other words, human beings must instinctively begin to act morally and compassionately towards one another, without compulsion or thought of reward. In biblical understanding, to act this way is to know the Hebrew Lord, such as in the book of Jeremiah, where the Hebrew Lord speaks to Israel, though His words apply to all peoples:

> "See, a time is coming"—declares the LORD [YHWH]—"when I will make a new covenant with the House of Israel and with the House of Judah. It will not be like the covenant I made with their fathers. . . . But such is the covenant I will make with the House of Israel after these days"—declares the LORD [YHWH]: "I will put My Teaching into their inmost being, and inscribe it upon their hearts. Then I will be their God, and they shall be My people. No longer will they need to teach one another, and say to one another, 'Heed the LORD [YHWH]'; for all of them, from the least of them to the greatest, shall heed Me"—declares the LORD [YHWH].[9]

6. Babylonian Talmud, *Sanhedrin* 98a.

7. Heschel, *Who Is Man?* 119.

8. Calaprice, *Ultimate Quotable Einstein*, 334, note: "From a conversation recorded by Algernon Black, Fall 1940. Einstein forbade the publication of this conversation." Einstein Archives 54-834. Princeton University Press, Princeton, NJ.

9. Jeremiah 31:31–34. JPS.

Salvation: Living *Olam* in This World

The Bible tells us that God wants the Jews to establish a society that sanctifies life as God-given and is concerned with the way people treat each other. In living this way, they are to be an example for all humanity. God tells Abraham that He will bless the nations of the world through his (Abraham's) descendants. In the Book of Isaiah, God says to the Jews, "I will also make you a light of nations, / That My salvation may reach the ends of the earth."[10]

The salvation of which God speaks must be in this world—the Hebrew Bible tells us of no other. It is therefore in people's lives. It is in living *olam.* The biblical God does not talk about life in heaven after death, which would make *this* life of secondary importance. On the contrary, in the book of Deuteronomy, God says to Moses, "I've put life and death in front of you. . . . You shall choose life, so you'll live, you and your seed."[11] To choose life, to live *olam,* is to do what the individual can do to bring about the golden age of universal love when God is fully real in the world and is recognized by all the world. In biblical times, this was considered a unique—and difficult—religious doctrine. It remains so today.

Other Religions Honor Life after Death

In contrast to the beliefs of ancient Hebrews, other religions offered people a way to escape the tribulations of life. On the popular level, Christianity and Islam say that suffering and injustice in this world will be compensated by an idyllic afterlife for those who deserve it. Though with far less emphasis, this belief also entered Talmudic Judaism.

The eastern religions, Hinduism and Buddhism, tend to turn inward, though there is no single philosophical principle that characterizes these beliefs. In general, classic Buddhism teaches you to handle life's problems from a detached perspective. A Hindu belief is that the body is different from the soul, so when problems cause pain, if you are enlightened you understand that it affects merely the body but not the soul, and you no longer suffer. Further, this life is just one of many you will lead, so if you do not achieve such enlightenment in this life, you may hope to do so in

---

10. Isaiah 49:6. JPS.

11. Deuteronomy 30:19. Friedman, *Commentary on the Torah.*

your next life. In an alternative view of detachment from physical life, *The Tibetan Book of the Dead* teaches that life itself is an illusion.[12]

We are so familiar with the widely held belief of "Life after Death" (as interpreted in Christianity, Islam, Hinduism, and Buddhism) that we tend to overlook how insidious such a lifestyle may be. "Life after Death" legitimizes acceptance of world injustices, evils, and unnecessary sufferings without necessarily requiring its followers to do much about them.

Mahatma Gandhi, for example, is universally admired as a Hindu saint (though his Hinduism includes aspects of Christianity), and he developed his system of *Satyagraha* in South Africa with his friends and closest allies, many of whom were Jews. Yet Gandhi's advice to the German Jews suffering under Hitler's heel was to let themselves be massacred. He wrote, "But if the Jewish mind could be prepared for voluntary suffering, even the massacre I have imagined could be turned into a day of thanksgiving and joy that God had wrought deliverance of the race even at the hands of the tyrant. For to the God-fearing, death has no terror. It is a joyful sleep to be followed by a waking that would be all the more refreshing for the long sleep."[13]

In current times, we are told that Islamic suicide terrorists blow themselves up along with their victims in the firm belief that they will be rewarded in paradise with many virgins. If there were no promise of such a compelling afterlife, however, we must ask if their actions in this world would be the same.

Ancient Hebrew religion confronts the world directly and seeks salvation within the world itself. It does not offer the solace of anything resembling a Christian or Muslim heaven. Yet the Bible tells us of the agony of the Hebrews when they were overcome in war and enslaved by their oppressors. Where, for them, was salvation in this world?

The question has not changed, even twenty-five hundred years later. Six million Jews were murdered in the Holocaust. Where, for them, was salvation in this world? We only find the Hebrew Lord's response to the sufferings of the ancient Hebrews, as He answers through His spokesmen, the prophets. In the book of Isaiah, the Lord says,

> Comfort, O comfort My people. . . .
> Fear not, My servant Jacob;
> Jeshuran whom I have chosen.

12. Sambhava, *Tibetan Book of the Dead.*
13. Gandhi, *Collected Works*, vol. 68, 139.

Even as I pour water on the thirsty soil,

And rains upon the dry ground,

So will I pour My spirit on your offspring,

My blessing upon your posterity.[14]

Well, what kind of response is *that*? Why should people in dire circumstances feel comforted just because sometime in the distant future, life will be great for their descendants?

14. Isaiah 40:1, 44:2–3. JPS. In the third line, the Hebrew text says "Jeshuran" is an alternate name for Israel.

11

The Hebrew Lord and "I"

The Messiah will come only when he is no longer necessary.

—FRANZ KAFKA[1]

LIFE WAS HARD IN ancient Israel. Like the peoples around them, the Hebrews often lived in wretched circumstances and experienced moments of great distress or suffering. Yet their lives were infused with a rich understanding of existence that spanned past, present, and future generations. That sense of *olam* allowed them to transcend time as "I am" while also understanding "I AM."

The Ancient Hebrew Rich Sense of Self

The ancient Israelite could be consoled by the Lord's words if he were able to identify his own being with the distant future. In other words, if his feeling of self could be extended to include the future, then he might derive solace in the present from these anticipated events.

Each of us tends to think of his own sense of self and instinct for self-preservation as ending at the boundary of the body. But when we have families and friends we love, most of us realize this is simply not true. Mothers and fathers are usually as concerned (if not more so) with the welfare of their young children as they are with their own.

In biblical days, such a sense of self widened to include the entire clan, and then entire peoples. The words of Isaiah and other prophets indicate that ancient Hebrews also extended their circle of self-concern into the distant future: "In the days to come, / The Mount of the LORD's House / Shall stand firm above the mountains / And tower above the hills / And all

1. Kafka, "Coming of the Messiah," 182.

the nations / Shall gaze on it with joy. . . . Nation shall not take up / Sword against nation; / They shall never again know war."[2]

Martin Buber, in interpreting the Bible, broadens the notion of self even further: "The Jewish Bible has always approached, and still does, every generation with the claim that it must be recognized as a document of . . . history, according to which the world has an origin and a goal. The Jewish Bible demands that the individual fit his own life into this true history, so that 'I' may find my own origin in the origin of the world, and my own goal in the goal of the world."[3]

Buber is saying that Jews of every generation find a sense of self by relating to the rest of humanity, not only within his lifetime but also with the peoples that came before him. His early visions and goals ultimately became his reality and in large part defined him as he continued advancing these goals by identifying what the world needed in his own time.

Spinoza's *aeternitas* may be described as a reaching of the self by expanding its perimeter in accord with the higher selfness of God. Development of the idea of *aeternitas* has, as its precedent, the biblical *olam*. This way of thinking may well have been easier for biblical Jews than it would be for us today, because it followed from their understanding of the world. Hebrew verb forms and other evidence in the Bible show us that to the ancient Hebrew, the past and future could be considered as real as the present. How different from today—and perhaps how insightful—these ancient people were in terms of their worldview, as well as in their concepts of self and time.

Einstein explains, in his theory of special relativity, that time is not an absolute and that the "here and now" must be considered in terms of an observer's point of view in space-time. This discovery, along with today's scientific knowledge that has emerged from it, are in harmonious agreement with the ancient Hebrew understanding that past, present, and future are all "real" and that each individual "I am" is not merely one lone self but an integral part of the Jewish identity and relationship to "I AM," now and forever.

That most people today have not subconsciously accepted the reality of past and future as an underlying aspect of their present reasoning, however, shows how difficult it is for a person to change his way of thinking. For example, the Passover *Haggadah* has retained this ancient

2. Isaiah 2:2, 2:4. JPS.
3. Buber, *Israel and the World*, 94.

understanding of self, expanded over time. Every year during the Passover seder, Jews recite the story of the biblical exodus from Egypt: "In every generation, every individual must feel as if he personally had come out of Egypt. As the Bible says: 'And you shall tell your son on that day, "It is because of that which God did for me when I came out of Egypt."' For it was not our ancestors alone whom God, blessed be He, redeemed. He redeemed all of us with them."[4]

Elie Wiesel has commented on this passage, regarding the notion of self across time: "First, the text does not say that every Jew must feel as if he had come out of Egypt. It says 'every individual.' And here we find the universal dimension of Jewish experience. After all, though the Torah was given to our people, have we not shared it with every other people? Second, the text says that every one of us must consider himself 'as if' he had come out of Egypt. Not, I did not leave Egypt, but I must think 'as if' I had been among those who did."[5]

This universality of experience and identity was also discussed by British Baptist pastor and scholar, H. Wheeler Robinson. He pointed to biblical evidence indicating that the Hebrew people looked upon themselves as a single entity, extending from the one to the many, into both past and future. This included those whose social status was higher than most others. Robinson explains, "To every other ancient monarch the subject was a slave; to the Israelite king he was a brother."[6]

More recently, another British pastor, Alec Gilmore, echoed Robinson's observations on the ancient people's "fluidity of thought" regarding self, "where words slide effortlessly between individual and community interpretations, so that either it is not clear which is being referred to, or the person speaking or writing seems to feel no need, or has no conscious desire, to make the distinction." In sum, he wrote, "Theirs was a world in which 'community' extended backward to embrace ancestors and forward to include generations yet unborn."[7]

From what I have come to know of the characteristics of these people and this language, I believe that the ancient Hebrews had a much richer sense of self than we have today. From their standpoint, our modern understanding

---

4. Exodus 13:8 in Wiesel: *A Passover Haggadah*, 68–69.

5. Wiesel: *A Passover Haggadah*, 68–69.

6. Robinson, *Corporate Personality*, 43.

7. Editor's note: See Gilmore, "Did Steinbeck Know Robinson?" 74.

of selfness—which we know as "a person's essential individuality,"[8] would indeed appear pitifully narrow and shallow.

The Self and Salvation

If today we could learn to expand our sense of what is real and enlarge our feeling of self in the ancient Hebrew manner, then we might be on our way to salvation, as understood in the sense of the Hebrew word *yaasa*, which means not only "rescue" but also "spaciousness" and "moving into the open."[9] This kind of salvation would take us from a rather narrow perception of reality to a broader one, just as our sense of self is evolving from "I am" to "I AM."

For example, Psalm 118:5 says, "Out of my straits I called upon YHWH; He answered me with great enlargement."[10] In other words, as I move from a restricted place, both physically and psychologically as a slave in Egypt and as still mentally limited as "I am," I may then cross the Red Sea to arrive safely in another place that is geographically open and theologically free.

I believe salvation thus requires enlargement of the feeling of self so that it extends outside the physical body to a greater spaciousness—a mindset that can, if biblical ethical precedents are followed, include the concerns of others. The enriched selfness would then bring an individual's "I am" closer to the "I AM" of God.

Speaking from a psychological viewpoint, William James concluded his Gifford Lectures over a century ago by saying that "the conscious person is continuous with a wider self through which saving experiences come."[11]

James does not attempt to explain the origin of this wider self, other than to suggest that it is "an altogether other dimension of existence from the sensible and merely 'understandable' world."[12] James' thought then is

---

8. Editor's note: *The Oxford English Dictionary* (www.oxforddictionaries.com/definition/english/selfness) and other modern dictionaries focus on the individual, notions of self-regard, self-centeredness, and selfishness. See also thefreedictionary.com/selfness and merriam-webster.com/dictionary/selfness.

9. Editor's note: Strong, *Strong's Exhaustive Concordance*.

10. Cohen, *The Soncino Chumash*, 289. The use of "enlargement" is unusual as the word is translated as "relief" in the JPS edition.

11. James, *Varieties of Religious Experience*, 505.

12. James, *Varieties of Religious Experience*, 506.

compatible with those psalms expressing intense personal suffering that is relieved with increased spaciousness—that is, when the mind of the psalmist opens to the presence of God.

> ## Everyday Steps in Expansion of the Self
>
> Each and every one of us, nearly every day, experiences changes in the margins of the self. Whenever we identify with another person, put ourselves in another person's place, experience sadness when confronted with another's pain, or rejoice at another's good fortune, we partially merge with another person's mind, thus sharing their subjective experience.
>
> —TODD E. FEINBERG, ASSOCIATE PROFESSOR
> OF NEUROLOGY AND PSYCHIATRY,
> ALBERT EINSTEIN COLLEGE OF MEDICINE[13]

Olam and the Expanding Sense of Self Today

Most of the time, a person is consciously aware of little more than his own physical body and his immediate surroundings. Through study, prayer, the way we act, and what we create, we try to elevate our thinking selves to embody a more expansive human reality—one that embraces others in the living past and the living future, as well as in the present—an elevation that reaches towards and opens to God. In biblical terms, we would call this reaching for *olam*.

The culture in which we live and the languages in which we think are very different from those of the biblical Hebrews. To reach toward *olam* may have been difficult for them, but for us it is even harder. One must think of selfhood as extending outside the physical body and reaching into past, present, and future. Yet we have the potential to sense the eternal *olam*, even in our modern lives—most easily when we love, help, and enrich the lives of others by what we do and what we create. But can *olam* be experienced today and actually provide comfort in today's world, even in times of intense suffering?

13. Feinberg, *Altered Egos*, 152.

One of the great documents of the Holocaust, less known than it should be, is the diary of Etty Hillesum, a young Jewish woman who was actively concerned with others and thoughtfully seeking meaning in life. At the time of the German invasion and occupation in 1941, she was a student in Amsterdam. She later worked for the Jewish Council and was then imprisoned along with her parents and brother in a Dutch deportation camp. In July 1942, she wrote,

> Living and dying, sorrow and joy . . . the persecution, the unspeakable horrors—it is all as one in me and I accept it as one mighty whole and begin to grasp it better if only for myself, without being able to explain to anyone else how it all hangs together. I wish I could live for a long time so that one day I may know how to explain it, and if I am not granted that wish, well, then somebody else will perhaps do it, carry on from where my life has been cut short. And that is why I must try to lead a good and faithful life to my last breath: so that those who come after me do not have to start all over again, need not face the same difficulties. Isn't that doing something for future generations?
>
> This sort of feeling has been growing much stronger in me: a hint of eternity steals through my smallest daily activities and perceptions. I am not alone in my tiredness or sickness and fears, but at one with millions of others from many centuries and it is all part of life.[14]

I believe Etty Hillesum found that precious, timeless *olam*, and that it provided her some degree of comfort. She died, aged twenty-nine, at Auschwitz in November 1943.

Judaism and the Expanding Self

The biblically inspired Jew seeks expansion of his "I am" to reach towards and open his mind to the "I AM" of the Hebrew Lord. The Jew seeks expansion of personal selfness into a fuller reality that includes the Jewish past and future. It is a reality in which doing the will of the Lord includes trying to mend the world, while absorbing both the sufferings and joys of life.

Jewish educator and theologian Israel I. Efros remarked that

> Judaism then is not a religion of rest. It does not stretch out its arms: Come to me, ye weary ones, and find rest. It is not a desire

---

14. Hillesum, *An Interrupted Life*, 130–1, 133.

for nirvana. . . . It is a deep experience and an endless going. It does not offer rest. Instead, it presents moral demands in which there is an idealistic longing for the impossible which is nevertheless a duty, as in the religious experience: Be ye holy for I am holy. It is a divine morality imposed upon a human creature, the infinite pressed into the finite.[15]

Efros's observations point to the responsibilities of Jews as well as to the rewards for living *olam*. But what of the actual, day-to-day suffering endured by Etty Hillesum and millions of other Jews? This could not simply be dismissed in favor of a better afterlife, as Judaism promises none.

Einstein's Greater Understanding of the Self

Albert Einstein sometimes received letters from families in pain who had suffered tragic personal losses and were asking for consolation. In the last years of his life, he replied with this standard letter:

> A human being is a part of the whole, called by us "Universe," a part limited in time and space. He experiences himself, his thoughts and feelings as something separated from the rest, a kind of optical illusion of his consciousness. This delusion is a kind of prison for us, restricting us to our personal desires and to affection for a few persons nearest to us. Our task must be to free ourselves from this prison by widening our circle of compassion to embrace all living creatures and the whole nature in its beauty. Nobody is able to achieve this completely, but the striving for such achievement is in itself a part of the liberation and a foundation for inner security.[16]

As Einstein showed in his own passionate protests against the social evils of his day, "widening our circle of compassion" meant actively seeking to improve human society, rather than passively accepting its present state. He wrote, "Whoever shuts his eyes to avoid seeing the bitter injustices of our times shares the guilt for their tragic continuation."[17]

15. Efros, *Ancient Jewish Philosophy*, 77. Efros taught at Johns Hopkins, University of Buffalo, and Hunter College, then became rector of Tel Aviv University.

16. Einstein letter to Norman Salit, March 4, 1950, Einstein Archives 61-226. Princeton University Press, Princeton, NJ.

17. Einstein letter about I. F. Stone's book, *Underground to Palestine*, October 27, 1946, Einstein Archives. Princeton University Press, Princeton, NJ. Encountered during Robert Goldman's research. Einstein was protesting Britain's forbidding of Jewish refugees to disembark in Palestine.

Inadvertently perhaps, Einstein was neatly paraphrasing Talmudic rabbis of two thousand years ago, who said, "He who can protest and does not, is an accomplice in the act."[18]

For the Jew to hold onto these ways for thousands of years in a usually hostile world has required stubbornness and the steadfast belief in expanding the sense of self to include Jews of the past and future (as they, too, define who we are now). The Jewish sense of self therefore also includes greater compassion for others, while attempting to right the wrongs of the world. If the Jewish people can continue to be "I am," and, in Isaiah's words, "a light unto the nations," they can do the will of the Hebrew Lord, while approaching and easing the way for the emerging evolutionary God, "I AM."

This evolutionary understanding is seen in the prophet Zechariah's observations, though he lived some 2,500 years ago: "'Return to Me,' says YHWH, 'that I may return to you.'"[19] Zechariah realized that all peoples of the Earth must think in terms of perfecting the world in order to bring about an age of true compassion for others. Thus the evolutionary God—the Hebrew Lord—may indeed emerge, and a golden age for humanity may be achieved.

18. Babylonian Talmud, *Sabbath* 54b.
19. Zechariah 1:3.

A Peculiar People

The remarks of eminent nineteenth-century French historian Ernest Renan (1823–1892) illustrate how Jews can be depicted with reasonable accuracy yet be thoroughly misunderstood:

> A peculiar people, in very truth, and created to present all manners of contrasts! This people have given God to the world, and hardly believe in Him themselves. They have created religion, and they are the least religious of peoples. They have founded the hopes of humanity in a kingdom of heaven, while all its sages keep repeating to us that we must only occupy ourselves with the things of this earth.[20]

Renan has unwittingly described what is close to the Hebrew Bible's ideal of religion. God's image cannot be produced, as is often done within Christianity. Rather than being seen, God wants to be understood, by having His ways in the hearts of all people, thereby shaping their actions. Truest religion is not to be found in ceremony but should be manifested in the nature of those actions, and the kingdom of heaven is not above the sky but rather a human kingdom emulating God's ways on Earth.

20. Telushkin, *Jewish Wisdom*, 501. Quoted in Almog, "Renan's Attitude to Jews," 258.

12

To Remove the Veil from Reality

Most mistakes in science and philosophy are made because
the image is taken for the reality.[1]

—ALBERT EINSTEIN

A FROG RESTS ON a lily pad in a sparkling lake at the foot of majestic, snow-clad mountains. Is the frog sitting contentedly admiring the surrounding scene? Four scientists at MIT answered that question over forty years ago in a classic paper they called, "What the Frog's Eye Tells the Frog's Brain."[2]

What the frog sees, the authors tell us, is not what you or I would see sitting on that lily pad. Its eyes can only detect moving objects—not stationary ones. The frog would starve to death if it were surrounded by food that was not moving. It can tell the difference between light and darkness, and it is keenly aware when a small object is moving fast across its field of vision. If attacked, it merely jumps from a light area into a dark area. Since the paper was written, scientists have learned that the frog can also detect and remember for about sixty seconds contours of large stationary objects, but little else.[3] The beauty of the world, the sparkle of the lake in which it sits, are beyond the frog's senses.

Wittgenstein's Impenetrable Veil

Inductive reasoning strongly suggests that on our higher level of being, the human level, the world's reality must also be fuller, richer in its extent and in depth, than we can detect with our senses. Even then, Einstein tells us,

1. Einstein, *Cosmic Religion*, 101.
2. Lettvin et al., "What the Frog's Eye Tells," 1940–51. Reprinted in McCullough, *Embodiments of Mind*.
3. David Ingle, letter to *New York Review of Books*, January 15, 2004.

today's methods of science are able to explore only part of that which we can detect: "The real is in no way immediately given to us. Given to us are merely the data of our consciousness; and among these data only those form the material of science which allows of univocal linguistic expression."[4]

Ludwig Wittgenstein was one of the most influential thinkers of the twentieth century. Two years before he died, after a lifetime of seeking truth and meaning through philosophical and linguistic analysis, he concluded, "What is eternal and important is often hidden from a man by an impenetrable veil. He knows: there is something under there, but he cannot see it. The veil reflects the daylight."[5]

To lift the veil completely would be to reveal the full, complete truth about the world, but we cannot yet understand it, as we are still limited by our senses.

Einstein's Walking Companion

In his last years, Albert Einstein lived within pleasant walking distance of the Institute for Advanced Study in Princeton, New Jersey. Kurt Gödel, his friend and associate at the Institute, lived a short distance away. In the mornings, Gödel would walk to Einstein's home on the way to the Institute, and together they would talk and walk the rest of the way. In an often-quoted remark, Einstein said that he went to work in the morning only because of this opportunity to talk to Gödel.

Kurt Gödel was one of the world's most brilliant logicians. As a young man, he published proof in 1931 that in any logically rigorous system, such as mathematics, there are truths that cannot be proved within the system. Commenting more recently, Leon Lederman, a Nobel laureate in physics, together with Christopher T. Hill, also a leading theoretical physicist, wrote, "This, at some point, must also carry implications for the enterprise of theoretical physics in any quest to finally reduce all of nature into a basic set of defining equations. It would naively seem to imply that there is always some experiment that can be performed with a definite outcome that cannot be predicted by the mathematics of theoretical physics."[6]

4. Einstein letter to Herbert Samuel, in Samuel, *Essay in Physics*, 158.

5. Wittgenstein, *Culture and Value*, 80. Wittgenstein wrote these words in 1949 and died in 1951. He'd been ashamed of his Jewish background in his younger years, as he sought truth in language, but he regretted that shame as he grew older.

6. Lederman and Hill, *Symmetry and the Beautiful Universe*, 75.

It seems inevitable that some perplexing questions in theoretical physics may never fit a mathematical structure or be answered, though each brings new questions to light. Even the methods of science, at least as we know them today, cannot fully lift the veil from reality.

A Question for Gödel

Gödel, concerned about his own mortality, was very interested in the concept of time. It is likely that he and Einstein talked about its mysteries on their frequent walks together. Einstein, you may remember, once exclaimed, "Nobody knows what time is anyway!"[7]

On Einstein's seventieth birthday, Gödel used some of Einstein's equations to construct a model universe in an essay dedicated to him. Gödel describes a model universe different from our own because it rotates rather than expands. In Gödel's universe, it would be possible—if you had a rocket ship capable of traveling close to the speed of light—to travel in a looping path into the past and return to the starting place, but earlier in time.[8] (Gödel, it later appeared, hoped that we did live in a universe that would permit such passage.[9]) Einstein called Gödel's model "an important contribution to the general theory of relativity, especially to the analysis of the concept of time."[10]

With this background in mind, I called Kurt Gödel and asked what he thought Einstein meant in the sympathy note he sent to Michele Besso's family upon his friend's death (mentioned in chapter six): "For us believing physicists, the distinction between past, present and future is only an illusion, even if a stubborn one."[11] Though I knew Gödel was famed for his reticence, I hoped he would expand on that statement.

7. Lederman and Hill, *Symmetry and the Beautiful Universe*, 75, footnote 146.

8. Gödel, "A Remark about the Relationship," in Schilpp, *Albert Einstein,* 555–62. Gödel's thesis about the possibility of travel into the past is discussed and defended by Horwich in *Asymmetries in Time*, 111–28.

9. After Gödel's death in 1978, pages of calculations were found among his papers, representing attempts to determine whether or not we did live in such a universe.

10. Gödel, "A Remark about the Relationship," Einstein's response to Gödel, in Schilpp, *Albert Einstein,* 687–8.

11. Quoted in Hoffman, *Albert Einstein*, 257–8.

But I was not at all prepared for the answer he gave me. After hesitating for a moment, his first words were, "I think he meant it as some sort of joke."[12]

Einstein joked often. But in his archives I had read many letters of condolence that he had written, and he did not joke in them. I cannot believe that Einstein, who knew at the time that he had not much longer to live, would write these words in jest to the family of his oldest friend.

Gödel continued, saying that Einstein believed that science could never explain consciousness: "The methods of science lead away from the life-world." He added that Einstein believed space-time to be a human construct—but reality was something deeper.[13]

Gödel's last statement is at the basis of both his and Einstein's beliefs: there is an ultimate reality—ultimate truth—that underlies our knowledge. Space-time is the arena of our history and our future—an arena in which we are consciously aware only of the passing present moment. Space-time itself does not represent reality but is a reduction from a fuller reality that remains hidden. Today's physicists agree.[14]

Reality can remain hidden even within scientific knowledge, as we are still ignorant of some things detectable at the quantum level; for example, if we try to measure where a particle is going, we cannot also know its location (Heisenberg's uncertainty principle). The best we can do is calculate the probability of a particle's location or momentum.

By the same token, we can only know some truths about our selves and our relationship to a Higher Self. But to do so is to dwell in *olam*.

---

12. Telephone conversation with Kurt Gödel, August 14, 1977.

13. Gödel was notoriously taciturn. I was able to speak directly to him on the telephone only because his wife, who usually answered the phone, was in the hospital at the time. Our conversation was just five months before his death from self-starvation, induced by a paranoid fear of food poisoning.

14. Editor's note: I believe Bob's discussion of ultimate reality here is a reference to Einstein's quest for a unified field theory; that is, a theory of everything, the Holy Grail in physics. In Bob's contact with Gödel, Einstein's letters, his secretary, and friends, Bob would have seen allusions to the key component of that ultimate truth, space-time. Just as did Einstein, though, Bob realized that space-time is only part of the answer to better understanding ourselves in relation to the universe.

We Can Participate in *Olam*

The Hebrew root of *olam* means "hidden." The eternal, *olam*, in its original Hebrew meaning, is veiled from us and may always be beyond our ability to comprehend. In biblical understanding, *olam*, full reality under God, is hidden from us, yet we can participate in it through our actions. A biblically based way of doing so is by expanding our feeling selves to include the pain and joy of others. Then, immersed in fuller reality, we act to reduce that pain, to increase that joy.

This understanding is fundamentally different from that of the ancient Greeks of the same period, which negates human reality. The Greek influence on Western culture is, of course, beyond measure. Twenty-five hundred years ago, Pindar, perhaps the greatest lyric poet of ancient Greece, wrote these lines:

> Creatures of a day.
> What is he?
> What is he not?
> A shadow in a dream is man.[15]

Plato, in *The Republic*, says the world of humanity is a shadow of reality—a reality in which we do not truly participate and which we cannot change. In the selection below, the parable of the cave, Socrates is talking to Plato's brother, Glaucon:

> And now I said, let me show in a figure how far our nature is enlightened or unenlightened—Behold! Human beings living in an underground den, which has a mouth open towards the light and reaching all along the den; here they have been from their childhood, and have their legs and necks chained so they cannot move, and can only see before them, being prevented by the chains from turning round their heads. Above and behind them a fire is blazing at a distance, and between the fire and the prisoners there is a raised way; and you will see, if you look, a low wall built along the way, like the screen which marionette players have in front of them, over which they show their puppets.
>
> I see.
>
> And do you see, I said, men passing along the wall carrying all sorts of vessels, and statues and figures of animals made of wood

15. Pindar, *Pythian Odes 8*, written to celebrate a wrestling victory in the 446 BCE Pythian games. Pindar lived from 518 to 438 BCE.

and stone and various materials, which appear over the wall? Some of them are talking, and others silent.

You have shown me a strange image, and they are strange prisoners.

Like ourselves, I replied: and they see only their own shadows, or the shadows of one another, which the fire throws on the opposite wall of the cave.[16]

The Platonic view is passive. The actions of men and women reflect a fate they cannot change. In contrast, the biblical view is active and hopeful. Humanity can strive to better its lot through the way people treat each other and in that manner more fully participate in a richer reality under God—in *olam*. Biblically, it is a reality that encompasses past and future. It is a reality that does not deny immediate human suffering, but comforts by diminishing its impact.

The biblical view, stated early in Genesis, is that God's creation is good—to increase knowledge of it is to increase knowledge of the good. This, then, is a view compatible with the scientific endeavor to extend our knowledge of reality with its mysteries of time and of self—an endeavor that can light the way to the Hebrew Lord.

Of Tomorrow's Hope, Tomorrow's Salvation

In the winter evenings of 1951, Einstein read the writings of thirteenth-century Jewish philosopher and physician Moses Maïmonides, who tried to explain the Hebrew Bible rationally in terms of Aristotelian philosophy, widely accepted at the time as the highest form of reasoning. Einstein noted how Maïmonides' thought was limited by the primitive scientific knowledge of his day. Seven hundred years from now, Einstein mused, people would find our present science as primitive as we consider the science of Maïmonides' time.[17]

In these pages, I have tried to show how rational reflection based on today's science can bring us closer to understanding the Bible's view of reality and its Hebrew Lord—an understanding often effectively hidden in translations from ancient Hebrew. But how would these ideas appear to a reader of this text seven hundred years from now?

16. Plato, *The Republic*, 253–4. The punctuation is Jowett's.

17. Einstein Archives. Princeton University Press, Princeton, NJ. Encountered during Robert Goldman's research.

The Nobel Prize–winning biochemist François Jacob wrote in 1973,

> Ultimately all organizations, all systems, all hierarchies, owe their very possibility of existence to the properties of the atoms described by Clerk Maxwell's electromagnetic laws. There are perhaps other possible coherences in descriptions. But science is enclosed in its own explanatory systems, and cannot escape from it. Today the world is messages, codes, and information. Tomorrow what analysis will break down our objects to reconstitute them in a new space? What new Russian doll will emerge?[18]

Today's science is progressing at a faster rate than ever before. We know only that seven hundred years from now, the veil over reality will be further removed—but in ways we cannot imagine.

More than two millennia ago, Isaiah proclaimed that in the golden age to come, the Hebrew Lord would fully remove reality's veil over us:

> He will swallow up the covering which is over all peoples,
> Even the veil which is stretched over all nations.
> He will swallow up death for all time,
> And YHWH will wipe tears away from all faces.[19]

For humanity to reach that golden age is the biblical hope. But we must work toward it. To achieve it, is to live *olam*.

18. Jacob, *The Logic of Life*, 324.
19. Isaiah 25:7–8. Jewish Publication Society, *The Holy Scriptures*.

Afterword

Etty

ESTHER "ETTY" HILLESUM LEARNED to live *olam* under the most horrific circumstances: the German occupation of Amsterdam, beginning in 1941.

A few miles away, Anne Frank was secretly writing the diary that made her famous. Etty Hillesum, less well known, also kept diaries—ten of her closely written notebooks survived—and she wrote many letters. In intimate terms, she discusses her inner questioning, her friends, her lovers, and her God.[1]

Etty was born in Holland in January 1914, the daughter of a classics professor, the grand-daughter of the chief rabbi of Holland's three northern provinces. She graduated from the University of Amsterdam, obtained a graduate degree in law, and then enrolled in the faculty of Slavonic languages. As do many youths today, she liked remaining in school. Her ambition was to be a writer.

At the time her diaries start, March 1941, Etty was twenty-seven years old, studying psychology on her own, earning a slim living by tutoring Russian, and working as a housekeeper in return for room and board. Her first diary entry reveals her initial materialistic view and suggests the start of her spiritual growth. She writes in that first entry, "I am accomplished in bed . . . and love does indeed suit me to perfection, and yet it remains a mere trifle, set apart from what is truly essential, and deep inside me something is still locked away."[2]

Hitler's troops had invaded the Netherlands nine months earlier. Aware of what to expect, Etty enters in her diary, "Everything will have to come more straightforward, until in the end, I shall, perhaps, finish up as an adult, capable of helping other souls who are in trouble, and of creating some sort of clarity through my work for others, for that's what it's really all about."[3]

1. Some of her writings, including diaries and letters, as well as photographs, can be seen in the Amsterdam Jewish Historical Museum.

2. Hillesum, *Etty*, 4 (March 9, 1941).

3. Hillesum, *Etty*, 14 (March 12, 1941).

Jews were continually being picked up by the German troops and taken to a Dutch transit camp, Westerbork. There, in a barbwire enclosure, they were held for later transport to the gas chambers of Auschwitz. No Jew knew when he or she would be sent to Westerbork. And while there, nobody knew when he or she would be put on the train to Auschwitz. Etty, while still in Amsterdam, philosophizes:

> If you have a rich inner life . . . there probably isn't all that much difference between the inside and outside of a camp. Would I myself be able to live up to such sentiments? There are few illusions left to us. Life is going to be very hard. We shall be torn apart, all who are dear to one another. I don't think the time is very far off now. We shall have to steel ourselves inwardly more and more. . . . I have the feeling I have a destiny, in which the events are strung significantly together.[4]

In Amsterdam, German persecution of Jews worsened, as Etty reports: "We are not allowed to walk along the Promenade any longer and every miserable little clump of two or three trees has been pronounced a park with a board nailed up: No admittance to Jews. More and more of these boards are appearing all over the place. Nevertheless there is still enough room for one to move and live and be happy and play music and love each other."[5]

The Germans continued to tighten their grip, adding more and more restrictions to Jewish life. One evening, with blistered feet from walking through the town because Jews weren't allowed to take public transportation, she writes,

> I am not bitter or rebellious, or in any way discouraged. I continue to grow from day to day, even with the likelihood of destruction staring me in the face . . . I have come to terms with life.
>
> By "coming to terms with life" I mean: the reality of death has become a definite part of my life: my life has, so to speak, been extended by death, by my looking death in the eye and accepting it, by accepting destruction as part of life and no longer wasting my energies on fear of death or the refusal to acknowledge its inevitability. It sounds paradoxical: by excluding death from our life we cannot live a full life, and by admitting death into our life we enlarge and enrich it.[6]

4. Hillesum, *Etty*, 279 (March 12, 1942).

5. Hillesum, *Etty*, 296 (March 22, 1942).

6. Hillesum, *Etty*, 463–4 (July 3, 1942).

The Nazis appointed a council made up of members of the Jewish community to aid in the transfer of victims to Westerbork. Etty disapproved of its tactics but wanted to ease the trip for the frightened victims. So she took a job with the council, shuttling between Amsterdam and the camp.

When her parents and brother were sent to Westerbork, Etty voluntarily went with them—this time to stay. She was now a prisoner at Westerbork. In her first letter to her friends in Amsterdam, she writes, "The misery here is quite indescribable. People live in those big barracks like so many rats in a sewer."

She tells of a train for Auschwitz being boarded:

> Early in the morning they were crammed into empty freight cars. Then another long wait while the train was boarded up. And then three days travel eastward. Paper "mattresses" were on the floor for the sick. For the rest bare boards with a bucket in the middle and roughly seventy people to a sealed car. . . . How many, I wondered, would reach their destination alive?

But in that same letter, she is able to philosophize:

> And yet, late at night when the day has slunk away into the depths behind me, I often walk with a spring in my step along the barbed wire and then time and again it soars straight from my heart—I can't help it, that's just the way it is, like some elementary force— the feeling that life is glorious and magnificent and that one day we shall be building a whole new world. Against every new outrage and every fresh horror, we shall put up one more piece of love and goodness, drawing strength from within ourselves.[7]

"The strength within ourselves" she attributed to God. Etty found the source of her knowledge of God deep within herself. In her words, "There is no hidden poet in me, just a little piece of God that might grow into poetry."[8]

In the Book of Exodus, at the burning bush, when Moses asks God his name, God explains that to the people of Israel He is "I AM."[9] An Israelite, then, is to relate to God through his or her own feeling of self-being, his or her own feeling of "I am." This understanding has carried over into the Jewish mystical system of Kabbalah. In Kabbalistic doctrine,

---

7. Hillesum, *Etty*, 615–6 (July 3, 1943).

8. Hillesum, *Etty*, 542 (October 3, 1942).

9. Exodus 3:14.

it is through a descent into one's own self that a person penetrates the spheres separating God from man.

Etty saw in helping others, in trying to reduce the intense suffering prevalent in Westerbork, a way of growing that piece of God within. Early in her diary she had entered the following: "I sometimes imagine that I long for the seclusion of a nunnery. But I know that I must seek You (God) amongst people, out in the world."[10]

Her outlook was harshly realistic. In a letter to an Amsterdam friend, she wrote,

> You know, if you don't have the inner strength while you're here to understand that all outer experiences are a passing show, as nothing beside the great splendor (I can't think of a better word right now) inside us—then things can look very bad here indeed. . . .
>
> People sometimes say, "You must try to make the best of things." I find this such a feeble thing to say. Everywhere things are both very good and very bad at the same time. The two are in balance, everywhere and always. I never have the feeling that I have got to make the best of things. Every situation, however miserable, is complete in itself and contains the good as well as the bad—
>
> All I really wanted to say is this: "making the best of things" is a nauseating experience.

But she believed that being forcefully separated from the ones they loved caused many inmates to suffer more than need be: "Most people here are much worse off than they need because they write off their longing for friends and family as so many losses in their lives, when they should count the fact that their heart is able to long so hard and to love so much among their greatest blessings."[11]

In her last weeks in Westerbork, Etty made the following entry in her diary: "You have made me so rich, oh God. . . . My life has become an Uninterrupted dialogue with You, oh God, one great dialogue. Sometimes when I stand in some corner of the camp, my feet planted on Your earth, my eyes raised towards Your Heaven, tears sometimes run down my face, tears of deep emotion and gratitude."[12]

And shortly before being put on the train for Auschwitz, she wrote to her old friend Maria Tuinzing:

10. Hillesum, *Etty*, 154 (November 25, 1941).

11. Hillesum, *Etty*, 637–8 (August 11, 1943).

12. Hillesum, *Etty*, 640 (August 18, 1943).

To My Little Maria,

How terribly young we were only a year ago on this earth, Maria!
And yet life in its unfathomable depths is so wonderfully good,
Maria—I have to come back to that time and again. And if we
just care enough, God is in safe hands with us despite everything,
Maria.[13]

Instead of blaming God for her predicament, she thought of God as
needing her help. Her attitude is remindful of the Hasidic riddle, "Where
does God dwell in the world?" And the answer is, "God dwells in the world
where Man lets him in."

According to Red Cross records, Etty Hillesum, twenty-nine years old,
died in Auschwitz on November 30, 1943. Etty showed us in her life that no
matter how difficult the circumstances, if we love others, if we do what we
can to alleviate suffering and help God perfect the world—then we are letting
light through the veil separating the world of humanity from fuller reality. We
let in light from the world of *olam*, where the Hebrew Lord dwells.

13. Hillesum, *Etty*, 657 (September 2, 1943).

Einstein's God:

Albert Einstein's Quest as a Scientist and as a Jew to Replace a Forsaken God

by

Robert N. Goldman

Goldman has had access to much unpublished correspondence bearing on what Einstein's remark, "I am a deeply religious non-believer" showed about him . . . an absorbing read on many levels.

—NEW SCIENTIST

I enjoyed the book very much and could hardly put it down. . . . Very valuable and deserves a wide readership.

—RONALD HENDEL

A fine exposition of a rarely considered dimension of Einstein's spiritual perceptions.

—W. GUNTHER PLAUT

New Scientist is Britain's leading journal of popular science. Ronald Hendel is professor of Hebrew Bible at the University of California, Berkeley. W. Gunther Plaut is past-president, the World Jewish Congress. He is editor and senior author, *The Torah: A Modern Commentary.*

Bibliography

Adler, Alfred. *Social Interest*. Oxford: Oneworld, 1998.

Alexander, Samuel. *Space, Time, and Deity: The Gifford Lectures at Glasgow, 1916–1918*. London: Macmillan, 1920.

Almog, Shmuel. "The Racial Motif in Renan's Attitude to Jews and Judaism." In Almog, *Antisemitism through the Ages*, 255–78. Pergamon, 1988.

Alter, Robert. *The Book of Psalms: A Translation with Commentary*. New York: Norton, 2009.

Amtzenius, Frank, and Tim Maudlin. "Time Travel and Modern Physics." http://plato. stanford.edu./archives/sum2000/entries/time-travel-phys/.

Aurobindo, Sri. *The Mind of Light*. Twin Lakes, WI: Lotus, 2003.

Avot, Pirkei. *Ethics of the Fathers*. New York: Hebrew, 1962.

Axelrod, Robert. *The Evolution of Cooperation*. New York: Basic, 1984.

Baclé, Louis-Lucien. *Future Life in the Light of Ancient Wisdom and Modern Science*. Chicago: McClurg, 1906.

Bar-Hillel, Yehoshua. "The Present Status of Automatic Translation of Languages." *Advances in Computers* 1 (1960) 91–163.

Barnett, Lincoln. *The Universe and Dr. Einstein*. New York: Morrow, 1948.

Barr, James. *Comparative Philology and the Text of the Old Testament*. Oxford: Clarendon, 1968.

Baum, Eric B. *What Is the Thought?* Cambridge, MA: MIT Press, 2004.

Bergson, Henri. *Creative Evolution*. New York: Modern Library, 1935, 1953.

Bermudez, Julio. *The Paradox of Consciousness*. Cambridge, MA: MIT Press, 1998.

Bleiweiss, Robert M., ed. *Torah at Brandeis Institute: The Layman Expounds*. Brandeis, CA: Tasmania, 1976.

Blood, Anne J., and Robert J. Zatorre. "Intensely Pleasurable Responses to Music Correlate with Activity in Brain Regions Implicated in Reward and Emotion." *Proceedings of the National Academy of Sciences* 98 (2001) 11818–23.

Born, Max. *The Born-Einstein Letters, 1916–1955: Friendship, Politics and Physics in Uncertain Times*. New York: Macmillan, 1971.

Brin, Ruth. *Harvest: Collected Poems and Prayers*. Duluth, MN: Holy Cow!, 1999.

Broch, Hermann. *The Death of Virgil*. New York: Pantheon, 1945.

Brockelmann, Carl. *Hebraische Syntax*. Neukirchen, Germany: Buchhandlung des Erziehungsvereins, 1956.

Brown, Francis, ed., with S. R. Driver and Charles A. Briggs. *A Hebrew and English Lexicon of the Old Testament*. London: Oxford University Press, 1951.

Buber, Martin. *Israel and the World*. New York: Schocken, 1963.

———. *On Zion: The History of an Idea*. Syracuse, NY: Syracuse University Press, 1997.

Calaprice, Alice, ed. *The Expanded Quotable Einstein*. Princeton, NJ: Princeton University Press, 2000.

———. *The Ultimate Quotable Einstein*. Princeton, NJ: Princeton University Press, 2013.

Camazine, Scott, Jean-Louis Deneubourg, Nigel R. Franks, James Sneyd, Guy Theraulaz, and Eric Bonabeau. *Self-Organization in Biological Systems*. Princeton, NJ: Princeton University Press, 2001.

Cassirer, Ernst. *Language and Myth*. New York: Harper and Brothers, 1946.

Celan, Paul. *Atemwende*. Frankfurt om Main: Suhrkamp, 1967.

Childs, Brevard S. *Memory and Tradition in Israel*. London: SCM.

Cohen, A., ed. *The Soncino Chumash*. London: Soncino Press, 1960.

Darwin, Charles. *The Origin of Species*. New York: Appleton, 1900.

Dawkins, Richard. *The Selfish Gene*. London: Oxford University Press, 1986.

De Vries, Simon John. *Yesterday, Today and Tomorrow: Time and History in the Old Testament*. Grand Rapids, MI: Eerdmans, 1975.

Descartes, René. *Discourse on Method*. New York: Barnes and Noble, 2004.

———. *Meditation III*. Translated by John Veitch, 1901. www.wright.edu/~charles.taylor/descartes/meditation3.html.

Durham, John I. "*Shalom* and the Presence of God." In John I. Durham and J. R. Porter, eds., *Proclamation and Progress* (Richmond, VA: Knox, 1970), 272–93.

Dyson, Freeman. *Infinite in All Directions*. New York: Harper and Row, 1988.

Efros, Israel I. *Ancient Jewish Philosophy*. Detroit: Wayne State University Press, 1964.

Einstein Archives. Princeton University Press, Princeton, NJ.

Einstein, Albert. *Cosmic Religion: With Other Opinions and Aphorisms*. New York: Covic-Friede, 1931.

———. "On the Electrodynamics of Moving Bodies." *Annalen der Physik* 17 (1905) 891–921.

———. *Out of My Later Years: The Scientist, Philosopher, and Man Portrayed through His Own Words*. Seacaucus, NJ: Citadel, 1973.

———. "Twin Paradox." https://en.wikipedia.org/wiki/Twin_paradox.

———. *The World as I See It*. New York: Philosophical Library, 1949.

Everyman's Library. *The Old Testament: King James Version*. London: Knopf, 1996.

Feinberg, Todd E. *Altered Egos: How the Brain Creates the Self*. New York: Oxford University Press, 2000.

Feynman, Richard P. *Six Not-So-Easy Pieces*. New York: Basic, 1997.

Freud, Sigmund. *Civilization and Its Discontents*. New York: Norton, 1989.

Friedman, Richard Elliott. *Commentary on the Torah*. New York: HarperOne, 2001.

———. *The Hidden Face of God*. New York: Harper Collins, 1995.

Galilei, Galileo. *Dialogue Concerning the Two Chief World Systems: Ptolemaic and Copernican*. Berkeley: University of California Press, 1953.

Gandhi, Mahatma. *The Collected Works of Mahatma Gandhi*. Vol 68. New Delhi: Publications Division, Ministry of Information and Broadcasting, 1976.

Georbran, Gevin. "Albert Einstein and the Fabric of Time." http://everythingforever.com/einstein.htm.

Gilmore, Alec. "Did Steinbeck Know Wheeler Robinson or His Theory of Corporate Personality?" *Steinbeck Studies* 15 (2004) 73–87.

Gödel, Kurt. "A Remark about the Relationship between Relativity and Idealistic Philosophy." In Paul Arthur Schilpp, ed., *Albert Einstein: Philosopher-Scientist*, 555–62 (New York: Tudor), 1951.

Goldman, Robert N. *Einstein's God*. Northvale, NJ: Aronson, 1997.

———. "Philip's Peril: Presenting a Puzzling Paradox of Person-ness." *Perspectives in Biology and Medicine* 16 (1972) 131–5.

Goldsmith, Maurice, Alan Mackay, and James Woudhuysen, eds. *Einstein: The First Hundred Years*. Oxford: Elsevier, 1980.

Gott, J. Richard III. *Time Travel in Einstein's Universe*. Boston: Houghton Mifflin, 2001.

Gould, Stephen Jay. "Kropotkin Was No Crackpot." *Natural History* 106 (1997) 12–21.

Groopman, Jerome. *The Measure of Our Days*. New York: Viking, 1997.

Halevi, Judah. *The Kuzari*. New York: Schocken, 1964.

Hawking, Stephen, Kip S. Thorne, Igor Novikov, Timothy Ferris, and Alan Lightman. *The Future of Spacetime*. New York: Norton, 2002.

Hermanns, William. *Einstein and the Poet: In Search of the Cosmic Man*. Brookline, MA: Branden, 1983.

Hertz, Joseph H. *Sayings of the Fathers*. Springfield, NJ: Behrman, 1995.

Heschel, Abraham Joshua. *God in Search of Man: A Philosophy of Judaism*. Northvale, NJ: Aronson, 1955.

———. *Moral Grandeur and Spiritual Audacity*. New York: Farrar, Strauss, Giroux, 1996.

———. *The Sabbath: Its Meaning for Modern Man*. New York: Farrar, Straus, Giroux, 1951.

———. *Who Is Man?* Stanford: Stanford University Press, 1965.

Hillesum, Etty. *Etty: The Letters and Diaries of Etty Hillesum, 1941–1943*. Grand Rapids, MI: Eerdsman, 2002.

———. *An Interrupted Life: The Diaries of Etty Hillesum, 1941–1943*. New York: Pantheon, 1984.

Hoch, James E. *Semitic Words in Egyptian Texts of the New Kingdom and Third Intermediate Period*. Princeton, NJ: Princeton University Press, 1994.

Hoffman, Banesh, with Helen Dukas. *Albert Einstein: Creator and Rebel*. New York: New American Library, 1972.

Horwich, Paul. *Asymmetries in Time*. Cambridge, MA: MIT Press, 1987.

Jacob, Francois. *The Logic of Life*. New York: Pantheon, 1973.

James, William. *The Varieties of Religious Experience*. New York: Random, 1929.

———. "The Will to Believe." In William James, *The Will to Believe and Other Essays in Popular Philosophy*, 1–3. (London: Longmans Green), 1907.

Jammer, Max. *Einstein and Religion: Physics and Theology*. Princeton, NJ: Princeton University Press, 1999.

Jenni, Ernst, and Claus Westerman, eds. *Theological Lexicon of the Old Testament*. Peabody, MA: Hendrickson, 1997.

Jerome, Fred. *The Einstein File: J. Edgar Hoover's Secret War Against the World's Most Famous Scientist*. New York: St. Martin's Griffin, 2003.

Jewish Publication Society. *The Holy Scriptures According to the Masoretic Text: A New Translation*. Philadelphia: Jewish Publication Society, 1955.

——— (JPS). *Tanakh: A New Translation of the Holy Scriptures According to the Traditional Hebrew Text*. Philadelphia: Jewish Publication Society, 1985.

Kafka, Franz. "The Coming of the Messiah." In Franz Kafka, *The Basic Kafka*, 182 (New York: Pocket), 1979.

Kahana, P'sikta D'Rav. Babylonian Talmud.

Kapitza, Pyotr (Peter) Leonidovich. *Experiment, Theory, Practice*. Dordrecht, Holland: Reidel, 1980.

Kaufmann, Walter. *The Faith of a Heretic*. New York: Doubleday, 1961.

Kluger, Rivkah Scharf. *Psyche and Bible*. Zürich: Spring, 1974.

Kopateh, Gil. *Haaretz Magazine*, Jerusalem (2005): 18–21.

Kosslyn, Stephen M. "2005: What Do You Believe Is True Even Though You Can't Prove It?" https://www.edge.org/response-detail/11826.

Kropotkin, P. *Mutual Aid: A Factor of Evolution*. London: Heinemann, 1902.

Kugel, James L. *The God of Old*. New York: Free, 2003.

Kuvakin, Valery Alexandrovich, ed. *A History of Russian Philosophy*. Vol. 2. Buffalo: Prometheus, 1994.

Laughlin, Robert B. *A Different Universe*. New York: Basic, 2005.

Lederman, Leon M., and Christopher T. Hill. *Symmetry and the Beautiful Universe*. Amherst, NY: Prometheus, 2004.

Lessing, Siegfried, ed. *Speculum Spinozum 1677–1977*. London: Routledge and Kegan Paul, 1977.

Lettvin, J. Y., H. R. Maturana, W. S. McCulloch, and W. H. Pitts. "What the Frog's Eye Tells the Frog's Brain." *Proceedings from the Institute of Radio Engineers* 47 (1959) 1940–51.

Levinas, Emmanuel. *Beyond the Verse*. London: Athlone, 1994.

———. *Difficult Freedom*. Baltimore: Johns Hopkins University Press, 1990.

———, ed. *Ethique et infini* (Ethics and Infinity). Paris: Le Livre de Poche, 1982.

Lichtenberg, Georg Christoph. *The Waste Books*. New York: New York Review of Books, 1990.

Lieber, David L., Jules Harlow, United Synagogue of Conservative Judaism, and The Rabbinical Assemby. *Etz Hayim: Torah and Commentary*. Philadelphia: Jewish Publication Society, 2001.

Marcel, Gabriel Honoré. *The Mystery of Being: Grandeur, Faith and Reality*, London: Harville, 1951.

Maturana, Humberto F., and Francisco J. Varela. *Autopoiesis and Cognition*. New York: Reidel, 1980.

Mayr, Ernst. *The Growth of Biological Thought: Diversity, Evolution and Inheritance*. Cambridge, MA: Harvard University Press, 1982.

———. "What Evolution Is: A Conversation with Ernst Mayr." Interview, December 31, 1999. https://www.edge.org/3rd_culture/mayr/mayr_index.html.

———. *What Makes Biology Unique?* Cambridge: Cambridge University Press, 2004.

McCulloch, Warren S. *Embodiments of Mind*. Cambridge, MA: MIT Press, 1965.

McGinn, Colin. *The Mysterious Flame*. New York: Basic, 1999.

McKenzie, John L. *The Two-Edged Sword: An Interpretation of the Old Testament*. Bruce, 1956.

Morgan, C. Lloyd. *Emergent Evolution*. London: Williams and Norgate, 1923.

Nadler, Stephen. *Spinoza: A Life*. Cambridge: Cambridge University Press, 1999.

Neusner, Jacob, and William Scott Green. *Dictionary of Judaism in the Biblical Period*. Peabody, MA: Hendrickson, 1999.

The New American Standard Bible (NASB). La Habra, CA: Lockman Foundation, 1995.

Nietzche, Friedrich. *Beyond Good and Evil: Prelude to a Philosophy of the Future*. Oxford: Oxford University Press, 2008.

Novikov, Igor D. *The River of Time*. Cambridge: Cambridge University Press, 1998.

Nuland, Serwin B. *The Wisdom of the Body*. New York: Vintage, 1997.

Pedersen, Johannes. *Israel: Its Life and Culture.* Oxford: Oxford University Press. Vols. 1-2, 1926; vols. 3-4, 1959.

Pfefferkorn, Eli, and David W. Hirsch. "Elie Wiesel's Wrestle with God." *Midstream* 43 (1997) 20–22.

Pindar. "Pythian Ode 8." https://chs.harvard.edu/CHS/article/display/5307.

Planck, Max. *Where Is Science Going?* New York: Norton, 1932.

Plastaras, James. *The God of Exodus.* Milwaukee: Bruce, 1966.

Plato. *The Republic.* New York: Modern Library, 1941.

Plutarch. *The Life of Theseus.* Plutarch's "Parallel Lives" series. http://penelope.uchicago.edu/Thayer/E/Roman/Texts/Plutarch/Lives/Theseus*.html.

Ponce, Charles. *Kaballah.* San Francisco: Straight Arrow, 1973.

Pringle-Pattison, Andrew S. *The Idea of Immortality: The Gifford Lectures Delivered in the University of Edinburgh in the Year 1922.* Oxford: Clarendon, 1922.

Rakic, Nataša. "Past, Present, Future, and Special Relativity." *British Journal of Philosophy in Science* 48 (1997) 257–80.

Ramachandran, V. S., and Sandra Blakeslee. *Phantoms in the Brain: Probing the Mysteries of the Human Mind.* New York: Harper Collins, 1999.

Raskin, Philip M. *A Book of Jewish Thoughts.* Oxford: Milford, 1920.

Riegel, Klaus F. "Time and Change in the Development of the Individual in Society." *Advances in Child Development and Behavior* 7 (1973) 81–113.

Robinson, H. Wheeler. *Corporate Personality and Ancient Israel.* Edinburgh: T. & T. Clark, 1981.

Rose, Steven. *Lifelines: Biology beyond Determinism.* Oxford: Oxford University Press, 1998.

Roth, Cecil, ed. *Encyclopedia Judaica.* New York: Macmillan Reference, 2006.

Sacks, Oliver. *The Man Who Mistook His Wife for a Hat.* New York: Touchstone, 1985.

Sambhava, Padma. *Tibetan Book of the Dead.* New York: Bantam, 1994.

Samuel, Herbert. *Essay in Physics.* Oxford: Basil Blackwell, 1951.

Saulez, William H. *The Romance of the Hebrew Language.* London: Longmans, Green, 1913.

Sayen, Jamie. *Einstein in America: The Scientist's Conscience in the Age of Hitler and Hiroshima.* New York: Crown, 1985.

Schilpp, Paul Arthur, ed. *The Philosophy of Rudolf Carnap.* La Salle, IL: Open Course, 1963.

Schofield, J. N. *Introducing Old Testament Theology.* London: SCM, 1964.

Science and Religion: A Symposium. London: Howe, 1931.

Scott, R. B. Y. *The Way of Wisdom in the Old Testament.* New York: Macmillan, 1971.

Searle, John R. *The Mystery of Consciousness.* New York: New York Review, 1997.

Shapiro, Fred R., ed. *The Yale Book of Quotations.* New Haven, CT: Yale University Press, 2006.

Shermer, Michael. "Macroscope: The Soul of Science." *American Scientist* 93 (2005) 101-3.

Shestov, Lev. *Na vesakh Iova* (On Job's Scales). Paris: Sovremennye zapiski, 1929.

Spinoza, Benedict de (Baruch). *Ethics.* London: Dent & Sons, 1989.

———. "Ethics: Demonstrated in Geometrical Order (Ethica, ordine geometrico demonstrata)." In Spinoza, *The Collected Writings of Spinoza* (Princeton, NJ: Princeton University Press), 1985.

———. *The Ethics and Selected Letters.* Indianapolis: Hackett, 1982.

———. *Short Treatise on God, Man, and His Wellbeing.* London: A. and C. Black, 1910.

———. *Spinoza: The Letters*. Indianapolis: Hackett, 1995.

———. *Tractatus Theologico-Politicus*. Leiden: Brill, 1991.

Spong, John Shelby. *The Hebrew Lord*. New York: Harper and Row, 1988.

Stern, J. P. *Lichtenberg: A Doctrine of Scattered Occasions, Reconstructed from his Aphorisms and Reflections*. Bloomington: Indiana University Press, 1959.

Strauss, Leo. *Persecution and the Art of Writing*. Chicago: University of Chicago Press, 1988.

Strong, James. *Strong's Exhaustive Concordance of the Bible*. Peabody, MA: Hendrickson, 2009.

Tagore, Rabidranath. *The Religion of Man*. Rhinebeck, NY: Monkfish, 2004.

Teilhard de Chardin, Pierre. *The Phenomenon of Man*. Glasgow: Collins, 1955.

Telushkin, Joseph. *Jewish Wisdom*. New York: Morrow, 1994.

Thorne, Kip S. *Black Holes and Time Warps*. New York: Norton, 1994.

Tolstoy, Leo. *A Confession, the Gospel in Brief, and What I Believe*. London: Oxford University Press, 1940.

Valera, Francisco J., Evan T. Thompson, and Eleanor Rosch. *The Embodied Mind*. Cambridge, MA: MIT Press, 1991.

Waldrop, M. Mitchell. *Complexity: The Emerging Science at the Edge of Order and Chaos*. New York: Simon and Schuster, 1992.

Wharton, Ken. "Lessons from the Block Universe." http://www.fqxi.org/data/essay-contest-files/Wharton_Wharton_Essay.pdf.

White, Andrew Dickson. *A History of the Warfare of Science with Theology in Christendom*. New York: Macmillan. 1898.

Wiesel, Elie. *Night*. New York: Bantam, 1982.

———. *A Passover Haggadah: As Commented Upon by Elie Wiesel*. New York: Simon & Schuster, 1993.

Wilson, Marvin R. *Our Father Abraham: Jewish Roots of the Christian Faith*. Grand Rapids, MI: Eerdmans, 1989.

Wittgenstein, Ludwig. *Culture and Value*. Oxford: Basil Blackwell, 1980.

———. *Notebooks, 1914–1916*. Oxford: Basil Blackwell, 1979.

Wouk, Herman. *This Is My God*. New York: Doubleday, 1959.

Yahuda, Abraham Shalom. *The Language of the Pentateuch and Its Relation to Egyptian*. London: Oxford University Press, 1932.

Yerushalmi, Yosef Hayim. *Zakhor*. Seattle: University of Washington Press, 1982.

Yovel, Yirimiyahu. *Spinoza and Other Heretics*. Vol 1: *The Marrano of Reason*. Princeton, NJ: Princeton University Press, 1989.

Index